UNHOOKED

UNHOOKED

STAYING
SOBER
AND
DRUG-FREE

J A M E S
CHRISTOPHER

PROMETHEUS BOOKS
Buffalo, New York

UNHOOKED: STAYING SOBER AND DRUG-FREE

Published by
Prometheus Books
700 E. Amherst Street, Buffalo, New York 14215,
800-421-0351; in New York State, 716-837-2475.

Library of Congress Catalog Card No. 89-62703
ISBN 0-87975-564-4

Manufactured in the United States of America.

DEDICATION

For Stephen Di Donna, my feisty nonalcoholic friend, who offered me reason, compassion, and support in my early sobriety, when I felt so alone and needed it the most—and for Tom and Dodie H., who have over seventy years of secular sobriety between them.

ACKNOWLEDGMENTS

This book is really the outgrowth of numerous caring, rational people, who through their unswerving support helped bring Secular Organizations for Sobriety into being: Dr. Paul Kurtz, Tim Madigan, Valerie Marvin, Dr. William L. White, Dr. Gerald LaRue, Mary Beth Gehrman, and John Winner.

I would especially like to express my gratitude to Robert Basil, my editor, who has been so helpful in encouraging me to expand this book. His efforts are deeply appreciated. I would also like to thank Larry Beck, who worked with me—at times for twelve-hour stretches—growing bleary-eyed in front of his computer screen, transforming my handwritten copy for this book into print.

Thousands of "secular sobrietists" have committed themselves to this grass-roots movement, rolling up their sleeves and starting their own autonomous SOS groups within their individual communities, nationwide and abroad. Perhaps the most exuberant convener of all is Janis Goodall, of San Francisco, California, whose efforts have spawned several SOS groups throughout northern California.

I am grateful.

TABLE OF CONTENTS

OTHER VOICES

INTRODUCTION

My name is Jim Christopher, and I'm forty-six years old. I am a sober alcoholic.

I drank for about seventeen years, with a seven-month "interruption" when I was thirty-one. At the age of thirty-five, on April 24, 1978, I again stopped ingesting the drug; and I have not drank alcohol or used any other mind-bending chemicals since that date. My sobriety has been continuous, daily. I have had no relapses.

Staying sober has given me a new life. Alcohol-related problems, with their "nightmare scenarios," are no longer mine in sobriety. Problems in living, however, *are* mine; I am an imperfect human being. But each new day is always a jewel. At this writing, with over eleven years of freedom from chemical dependency, I now can experience myself and my life in *real* ways. My circumstances are not always pretty—but, again, in comparison to my drinking years, especially those later drinking years, my worst day in sobriety outshines my "best" day lived "under the influence"—when I slept in my own vomit, stumbled through blackouts, and generally relinquished my life to alcohol.

I am *unhooked*. And today I work with others in helping them get unhooked—through my own one-on-one counseling practice and by fostering the SOS movement. SOS stands for Secular Organizations for Sobriety. It also stands for Save Our Selves. Hundreds of SOS groups have developed in the past three years. This book tells the story of how this radical, new approach to addiction-recovery has helped thousands get off booze and drugs, helped them when traditional programs have failed. The program is radical in its simplicity—in what it *leaves out*. There's no dogma, no appeals to the "higher power" revered and feared by Alcoholics Anonymous.

Unhooked will describe this new program. You will also meet dozens of people who have begun their recovery through SOS. Indeed, I leave most of the latter half of *Unhooked* to these poignant voices. They are passionate and individualistic, and they are sober.

MY BACKGROUND

I was raised in a fundamentalist family. I was an only child, raised in Texas, a Baptist. At one point I was a believer.

Early on, I suppose, I was indoctrinated, as most children are in religious families, into my parents' beliefs. I was not a tongue-speaker, but neither my parents nor my church frowned on such practices. Anything was great as long as it put you in touch with God (or, as I would say now, with the "bicameral mind").

In my family, the rational part of living was secondary to the *believing* part of living. That's what they stressed, mainly. With the believing came strong feelings: the crying, the emotions, which are a very important part of belief. But then there was also the fear and the guilt: You are a sinner, you were born into sin.

How devout a believer was I? I was very fearful, so I was *very* devout. I remember once—I think I was a preteen—I was in the family car and my parents got out to do some shopping. When they didn't return for a long time, I thought they had been taken up in "the rapture" and I had been left behind. This is a kid thinking, and what sins can a kid commit? I mean, I didn't have a criminal history or anything, but I was obsessed with all my "kiddy" sins, so I thought I had been left behind. I really went into a panic.

My father is dead now. He was the more easygoing of my parents. My mother is still quite into her religious life. We haven't been in touch with each other for several years. I underwent a process whereby I "divorced" my mother; I think it can be healthy for people to do that. I have nothing against her right to be her, but I have a right to be me.

I only bring up my family as a way of stressing that such family issues *don't matter as far as keeping sober goes.* Your Ma might have hit you with a frying pan back in the thirties in Dubuque, but that doesn't have much to do with your life now. That's not why you are an alcoholic. Alcoholics and non-alcoholics drink for the same reasons; people become alcoholics because they can get chemically *hooked.* You can be predisposed to alcoholism and never become an alcoholic. You could have been raised not to drink, or have been convinced not to by being witness to alcohol's harmful, frequently deadly effects. So, if nature doesn't keep you off, sometimes "nurture" will.

But if you are genetically predisposed to alcoholism, and you start to drink, you are going to become addicted, *enslaved,* as I was in my late teen years.

The Bad News: You might never get over the feeling of that swinging frying pan.

The Good News: You don't need to, in order to escape the hellof your active addiction. Having a wonderful life (and thinking pure thoughts) are not prerequisites for sobriety, thank goodness.

There is no such thing as an "alcoholic personality." Researchers have found that problems in life are *exacerbated* by drinking, but problems don't bring on "cellular thirst." Neither does "moral weakness."

THE TRADITIONAL PROGRAMS

Most addiction-recovery programs—both in-patient and out-patient—are derived from the philosophy of Alcoholics Anonymous, or AA. The basics of the AA program are put forth in its famous "Twelve Steps," contained in the so-called *Big Book,* the "Bible" of AA.

AA insists that its program and precepts are "spiritual," not religious. But there are a lot of people who cannot relate to AA's version of spirituality, or who don't consider themselves religious or "spiritual" at all. They have a hard time believing that faith in the supernatural is a prerequisite for sobriety. Indeed, even religious believers who don't understand why faith should guarantee—or subvert—sobriety have felt uncomfortable within AA. Are the lives of these people any less important than the lives of spiritual or religious people? Shouldn't there be a program designed for them, too?

*   *   *

Here is the heart of the program of Alcoholics Anonymous:

> Without help [our alcoholism] is too much for us. But there is One who has all power—that One is God. May you find him now!
>
> Half measures availed us nothing. We stood at the turning point. We asked His protection and care with complete abandon.
>
> Here are the steps we took, which are suggested as a program of recovery:
>
> 1. We admitted we were powerless over alcohol—that our lives had become unmanageable.
>
> 2. Came to believe that a Power greater than ourselves could restore us to sanity.
>
> 3. Made a decision to turn our will and our lives over to the care of God as we understood Him.
>
> 4. Made a searching and fearless moral inventory of ourselves.
>
> 5. Admitted to God, to ourselves, and to another human being the exact nature of our wrongs.
>
> 6. Were entirely ready to have God remove all these defects of character.

7. Humbly asked Him to remove our shortcomings.

8. Made a list of all persons we had harmed, and became willing to make amends to them all.

9. Made direct amends to such people wherever possible, except when to do so would injure them or others.

10. Continued to take personal inventory and when we were wrong promptly admitted it.

11. Sought through prayer and meditation to improve our conscious contact with God as we understood Him, praying only for knowledge of His will for us and the power to carry that out.

12. Having had a spiritual awakening as the result of these steps, we tried to carry this message to alcoholics, and to practice these principles in all our affairs . . . , our personal adventures before and after make clear three pertinent ideas:

   (a) That we were alcoholic and could not manage our own lives.

   (b) That probably no human power could have relieved our alcoholism.

   (c) That God could and would if He were sought.[1]

Let me say that legions of individuals have benefited from these precepts. Any honest observer, though, must also admit that legions of individuals have fallen away from AA.

Why? Because they can't "work the program." And then there are the many who keep quiet, who take from AA what they can use, retranslating (or ignoring) the rest to fit their individual purposes, and survive.

Please remember that one comes to a program of recovery—any program of recovery—reaching out for help, when one is most vulnerable. This does not mean, however, that one needs to sacrifice one's intellectual integrity or compromise one's individuality in order to achieve and maintain a life of sobriety.

People who have studied religions and cults have found again and again that people tend to convert at times of great stress or failure in their lives. These are the times when promises of enlightenment and cures for pain are most appealing. We don't look for proof or evidence or even coherence in belief. We see somebody throwing us a life-preserver and we grab it. Put in this context, we can see why the religious fervor that permeates AA's meetings and literature could go unchallenged for so long.

When you've lost faith in yourself, it's only too easy to find it in anything else.

RELIGIOUS THINKING

What is the source of the religious mind?

Many philosophers, biologists, and psychologists now hypothesize that mankind's religious thinking is a powerful vestige of the early days of our species. In *The Origins of Consciousness in the Breakdown of the Bicameral Mind,* Julian Jaynes speculates that only until relatively recently in human history have the right and left hemispheres of our brains been fully connected with each other. We had the same "equipment" as our forbears—it just wasn't used the same way. When their right hemisphere communicated with their left, its "voice" sounded as though it was coming from someplace else. In short, humans believed these voices were the commanding voices of gods. In a sense, these early humans were not truly conscious. While most of us are no longer "bicameralized"—psychotics and New Age "channelers" excepted—there lingers in our cultural DNA the yearning to find, and to obey, an all-powerful "voice." That's according to Jaynes's theory.

Similarly, E. O. Wilson in *Sociobiology* argues that there might well be a genetic predisposition to believe. According to Wilson, tribes that believed in gods were perhaps more successful in reproducing their kind than were "atheistic" tribes. Is there a religious gene, then? The jury is still out. But there certainly is something that Paul Kurtz calls the "transcendental temptation"—an innate urge to believe, if not in the gods of the traditional religions, then in all manner of paranormal phenomena of today: UFOs, astral bodies, and so forth. The ability to reason has been gained by our species only recently. Obviously, the urge to escape from it can be strong.

I think, however, that it is an unwise move for the sober alcoholic to return to the bicameral mind, to religious superstition of the kind often found in AA. We want to stay in touch with who we are. We need to remain fully conscious and aware of what's going on inside our heads. There is no evidence that higher powers are going to come down from heaven and save us. We have to look out for ourselves. And to do that, we need to keep our eyes open.

Ah, yes, but what about the "spiritual"? Don't we need some kind of emotional inspiration? Of course we do, but it need not be religious. We can still enjoy the power of our imagination. We can experience a sense of exhilaration, exuberance, and meaningfulness without resorting to magical thinking. Our dreams of what can be, within the realm of the natural world (and that's a pretty big realm), can be freed up through sobriety, to soar to new undrugged heights. We can fully appreciate our individual power through sobriety.

Not long ago, I traveled to meet a man whose work in

the field of alcoholism I greatly admired. The meeting, unfortunately, did not go well. Together with an openly hostile colleague, he cornered me in a heated grill-fest over coffee. I'd expected civility and a stimulating exchange of ideas. Astonishingly, and insultingly, both of them denied my sobriety, not to mention the sobriety of legions of others who had "recovered without religion."

> She (holding forth): "Where does love come from?"
> Jim: "From us."
> She again: "Where do we come from? What's the meaning of life, if there's not something out there greater than ourselves?"
> He: "Well, she hasn't read your book. But really, without a 'spiritual connection,' one tends to be in danger of creating another Jonestown." (He was referring, of course, to the late Jim Jones, who, via hallucinations—aided by beliefs and designer drugs—revealed to the world a darker side of "spirituality." He also informed me that physicists saw not chaos but "a force, some unnamed power 'behind' it all." He even told me that quarks were spiritual.)
> She (questioning my longterm sobriety): "Haven't you had a relapse?" (meaning "How the hell does a purely secular soul like yourself stay sober?")

One becomes used to this kind of encounter: "How dare you be sober 'n' happy without my Lord, my esoteric insights, or my one hand clapping?"

I dare to be, and I am.

THE HEROIN CONNECTION

One reason myths like "the alcoholic personality" have been popular over the years is because medicine simply didn't know that much about the biology of alcoholism. Since there were no *obvious* physical differences between alcoholics and nonalcoholics, the difference was thought to be found in their personalities—or so, unfortunately, the thinking has gone in AA. And so, often tragically, alcoholics have had to contend with feelings of acute shame and self-doubt on top of their addiction.

We now know, though, that alcoholics differ from nonalcoholics in key *biological* ways:

1. The levels of a substance called acetaldehyde that is found in the bloodstream. Although acetaldehyde is a normal by-product of alcohol metabolism, alcoholics produce much higher levels than nonalcoholics.

2. The presence in the brain of a highly addictive, heroinlike substance called TIQ (tetrahydroisoquinoline), which many feel is the root cause of alcoholic addiction. It is found in high levels in the brains of alcoholics.

3. The thickening of the brain cell membranes. These membranes are abnormally thickened in the brains of alcoholics and require constant supplies of alcohol to function "normally." If alcohol is withheld, the membranes work badly and the body experiences intense discomfort or withdrawal. The membranes do not feel "normal" until alcohol is again ingested.[2]

These discoveries were happened upon in an interesting way. In 1979,

Dr. Virginia Davis of the Veteran's Administration was examining the brains of recent cadavers from the Skid Row area of Houston. She found a substance in their brains usually found only in heroin users, and she associated these men with drug addiction.

However, when she discussed this with the Houston police, they pointed out that the men were "winos" who could never have afforded heroin. Upon further investigation, Dr. Davis discovered that alcohol had combined with dopamine to produce the addictive substance TIQ, whose effects within the brain were almost identical to those of heroin.

Subsequent studies of live alcoholics confirm these findings. TIQ has been found in the urine of alcoholics, but not in the urine of the control group of nonalcoholics.[3]

The ramifications of this research are important for peer-group counseling groups. If alcoholics are biologically *predisposed* to an addiction as tenacious as *heroin* addiction, then they need to focus first and foremost on *sobriety itself*. To focus instead on the "personality flaws" that allegedly bring on alcoholism is to miss the point of this current research.

THE BREAK

When I started to recover from alcoholism, AA was there. There was nothing else.

Still, before I got sober I was leaning toward humanism. But when I came into AA, I was questioning my ideas about everything. After all, I felt as though I had failed in life: I was an addict. Hence all my thinking was open to revision. And AA said that belief in a higher power was the answer. So I tried to believe, to go back to my youth, to create a "kinder, gentler" God.

But after I had been sober for awhile, I began to ask questions: What exactly *was* God's will? And there were people in AA willing to confidently answer that question, believe it or not. They were like priests, and they felt they could mediate personally between me and the supreme being. "Do as I say," they said, "or else you'll lose your sobriety." That's a powerful threat.

As the years passed, however, I would interview long-term

sober people. Why had they remained sober? What was the key? Did they have some spiritual conversion? Some felt as though they did, but a good many felt otherwise.

Indeed, the single quality that united all these long-term sober alcoholics was not religious at all. They stayed sober because they didn't even think of drinking; they saw their sobriety as an issue separate from everything else in their life. It wasn't connected to their friends, to their finances, to their jobs, or even to their moods. That was the common thread.

In my third year of continuous sobriety I began to pull away from Alcoholics Anonymous. And that was scary for me. During this early transition period I started attending discussion meetings of a then-tiny atheist organization, held in a local library.

The no-name band of atheists was in the midst of political change, severing its connections with America's most controversial, cantankerous atheist, Madalyn Murray O'Hair. I knew nothing of these internal political machinations. At that point I wasn't even comfortable with the term "atheist." I was, however, in the process of attempting to grow in my sobriety, to free myself from questionable dogma, and to find secular persons of like mind (both sober alcoholics and nonalcoholics) to relate to in this process.

The group began meeting in a larger facility in a neighboring beach community, Marina del Rey. I attended an early "formation meeting" there, and the group was larger, and a little more diverse: atheists, agnostics, humanists, skeptics, and assorted freethinkers. After several informal yet passionate podium pronouncements from the organizers, the floor was thrown open to all of us. The voices were strident.

"We should call ourselves something that really reflects who we are: Atheists, with a capital 'A.' None of this pussyfoot bullshit!" said one dark-haired, fist-shaking fellow from the back of the room.

Another chimed in: "The Catholics and other religionists have controlled this country for long enough!"

A lady rose from her folding chair and proclaimed, "It took years of psychotherapy to free me from that crap!"

But one white-haired gentleman, barely able to stand, offered, "We can work together, extend a bridge of understanding and friendship, especially to those in the liberal religious community. We've all got to live together; let's not make the mistake of alienating our friends. I'm not only a Unitarian and a secular humanist, I'm also a human being."

And so it went.

I was nervous, but stood to speak nonetheless: "My name is Jim Christopher and I'm a sober alcoholic." I heard a couple of moans. I continued: "AA doesn't meet the needs of all people, and I feel that there should be a secular alternative. . . . "

A bearded guy cut me off: "This is an *A*-theist meeting. Not a meeting to discuss alcoholism or any other unrelated topic. We've gotta keep a focus here. All these other things are beside the point!"

I sat down, a bit shaken. Heated rhetoric continued. Numerous names were proposed for the no-name group: "Atheist Community," "Atheists Together," "Atheists Triumphant," and so on. (The bitterness and bravado I found there was typical of such groups, I later discovered.)

After the meeting, as I was browsing at the literature table, attended by a delightful lady who referred to herself as a "born-again atheist," I was approached by two younger guys. One said, "We liked your idea. AA is pretty heavy on the religious bit."

His friend asked, "Do you still attend AA meetings?" I replied that I hadn't been attending very often recently, and that I hoped to help start some sort of alternative meeting for alcoholics within the freethought community. They encouraged me to "hang in there," and left.

Before I could turn back to the literature table, a chubby fellow extended his hand, introduced himself, and asked if I'd like to be on a mailing list for literature that explained "the gross exaggerations regarding the Holocaust during World War II." Stunned, I told him that I really wasn't interested in fascist fantasies, and he retreated, glad-handing the next body in sight. As I perused the magazines and pamphlets, it dawned on me that although Hitler and Mussolini had been Christians, the jerk I'd just encountered was testament to the fact that some atheists could be lunatics (or worse) as well, as fanatical as revival preachers, spewing hatred under another banner. But by and large I had generally found most freethinkers to be tolerant and level-headed. Secular folks seemed more apt to "live and let live" than most religious persons, especially those whom I'd encountered in the Baptist burn-in-hell background of my youth.

I flipped through various publications and took note of one magazine entitled *Free Inquiry,* as well as a small newspaper, *Freethought Today.* I took a Prometheus Books brochure with me, then I walked out of the building past bronzing sun-worshipers, their bodies clad in screaming pinks and greens, set against the deep blue of the marina.

THE MOVEMENT BEGINS

I started to correspond with the organizations I learned about at the no-name atheist meeting. *Free Inquiry* magazine proved to be a wonderful source of information regarding the scope of the humanist community. Through it I learned of its affiliated organization, the Committee for the Scientific Investigation of Claims of the Paranormal (CSICOP), publishers of a fascinating quarterly called *The Skeptical Inquirer.* I also joined the Freedom from Religion Foundation (headquartered in Madison, Wisconsin) and began receiving their monthly newspaper, *Freethought Today.* I ordered a number of books through the Prometheus Books catalogue and anxiously awaited their arrival by mail. When the box from Buffalo came, I devoured works on philosophy, ethics, science, humanism, religion, and freethought. My favorite was *Exuberance: A Philosophy of Happiness,* by secular humanist philosopher Paul Kurtz. I learned that Dr. Kurtz was the publisher of Prometheus Books and the editor of *Free Inquiry* magazine.

This was an exhilarating time for me, as I began to re-embrace my secular leanings, my humanism, thoughts that I had secreted away in a corner of my mind during my early sobriety. Why had I repressed these ideas for so long? I suppose it was to surrender what fellow AA members called "your mind, which is killing you." They used to say, "Your best thinking is what got you where you were." What they meant, ultimately, was: "Don't rock the boat of the AA philosophy; don't doubt the 'Higher Power,' or you'll surely drink again."

But I challenged these precepts. I was filled with my own thoughts and feelings, and began to experience an amplified sense of my own power in sobriety. I wept openly in my joyous liberation. Meanwhile, back at the marina, "Atheists United" had formed and I began attending regularly. There were some really caring people there; the small antisemitic faction had been booted out in an explosion of unanimous outrage. We had a good, healthy group.

I should digress, and admit that this wasn't the first group I had joined. At the end of my first year of sobriety I got caught up in a "spiritual" teaching—a church really—called "Science of Mind." Fellow AA members turned me onto this philosophy, an offshoot of Mary Baker Eddy's Christian Science movement. This church was a fad among many of my AA buddies at the time, and I really got into it, too, "treating" (or "healing") myself of "wrong" (i.e., *real*) thoughts regarding life and disease. With hands extended, palms heavenward, I was encouraged in classes to believe that one could give "a treatment" to secure a parking place in a crowded lot, to reverse any disease or other "illusionary" process, and to "avoid victimization." (We believed that if a mugger beat the hell out of you, it was really *your* fault for having put yourself in such a position.)

Soon after I received my certificate from Science of Mind, two fortuitous events jolted me out of the New Age and back into reality. I'd advanced so far into loony-land that an annoyed nonalcoholic New Yorker friend could take no more of my "spirituality." In his strong, no-nonsense Bronx-accented voice, he said, "If you ask me, coming from 'the city,' if you're going to entertain the idea that there are no such things as victims in this life, you gotta be mad as a hatter!" His straightforward approach shook some mental screws loose, allowing the fresh air of reason through to my "spiritually" muddled brain.

Then I met a fellow who'd previously been sober for five years, during which time he'd also become deeply involved in Science of Mind. He told me that he'd "treated" himself for the removal of the "false disease idea of alcoholism." He said he could "drink socially" again. Of course, his chemical dependency reasserted itself; his "treatment" took him into a full-blown relapse, complete with a hospital stay, where he required detoxification and life-saving measures for an alcohol-related heart problem. His candid revelation blew loose the remaining "spiritual" screws from my skull, freeing me again to think for myself in sobriety.

*   *   *

In my work over the years as an advertising sales director for newspapers, ad agencies, and periodicals, I'd written numerous articles and advertising copy for clients. Later, after gaining some rationality in my sobriety, I decided that it was time to write an article about my frustrations with AA and to submit it to *Free Inquiry* magazine. I discovered that Paul Kurtz would be in town in early 1984 for a *Free Inquiry* conference at the University of Southern California. I attended with some freethinking friends from my local Unitarian church, and brought an envelope with me containing a short article I'd written, entitled "Sobriety Without Superstition." I approached Dr. Kurtz after his talk, thrust the envelope into his hand, mumbled a few words and returned to my seat in the auditorium.

Later, in February, I received a brief letter accepting the article for publication in *Free Inquiry*. When "Sobriety Without Superstition" eventually appeared in the summer of 1985 I was delighted, but I was unprepared for the tremendous response it evoked from readers across the country. I had struck a nerve. Thousands of people had been thinking the way I was, and desired an alternative to AA. So there was a lot of work to do. More articles for *Free Inquiry, Freethought Today,* and other publications were soon to follow; and as I continued to write, I began receiving invitations to speak at Unitarian-Universalist churches, atheist and humanist groups, the local Ethical Cultural society, and other organizations within the freethought community.

During one question-and-answer period after a talk at a small Unitarian church, a lady in the audience asked, "Why can't there be a *secular* meeting? I'm a recovering alcoholic and AA groups are driving me crazy with all that 'God Stuff.' I'm staying sober, been sober for four years, but no matter which meetings I attend, this 'Higher Power' dogma is pushed as a requirement for sobriety. Like you, Jim, I know that this is simply not true. Are there any alternative meetings anywhere? I'm willing to drive—I drove forty miles to this talk today." I told her that I knew of no such meetings. "Why don't you start one, then?" she asked.

I did—after my attempts to begin a secular group *within*

AA were soundly rejected. I began the first group in November of 1986, in North Hollywood, California, where I'd moved to a new apartment and a new job. The first days of the Secular Sobriety Groups (as SOS was then called) are recounted in *How to Stay Sober: Recovery Without Religion,* which I wrote as the new groups and the secular recovery movement progressed.

Today, only a little over two years later, there are grass-roots groups in all fifty states as well as in Canada, Europe, and Australia. SSG is now SOS—Secular Organizations for Sobriety and Save Our Selves—and it is providing a hearty alternative to AA, whenever and wherever those who feel there is a need for SOS also have the willingness to start these peer-group counseling groups.

SOS groups connect with each other by way of a national newsletter. The grass-roots meetings are free of charge, self-supporting, and conducted on an anonymous basis. Each group is autonomous. These are the prerequisites: that groups exist in order to provide peer support for alcoholics (as well as for those addicted to other mind-altering drugs) who want to achieve and maintain continuous sobriety; that meetings are meant for sober alcoholics/addicts to share the thoughts and feelings they have regarding their recovery; and that the atmosphere is *nonreligious.*

WHAT YOU NEED TO KNOW

What is "cognitive sobriety"?

"Cognitive" means *knowing, learning, insightful.* You look at the world and your life in a rational way and try to know what the dynamics behind things are. The Reagan philosophy of "just saying no" doesn't help people very much. How could it? You need to know *how,* and you want to know *why.* Simple-minded slogans don't fulfill these basic human yearnings. Perhaps the pervasive repetition of that kind of slogan will convince a few that it is no longer popular to get ripped; then again, perhaps its dogmatic, self-righteous tone will have the opposite effect.

Traditional therapies, usually based on AA's twelve-step model, connect sobriety to God. New Agers or proponents of what is called "transpersonal therapy" would connect it to some mystical "unity" or "cosmic holism."

Even those who are more rational often say, "If you get *good,* you can get sober."

Others will say, "Well, you have to learn 'coping strategies,' and you have to alter your life here, and you have to take these certain steps to do such and such." All these things might very well be valuable and important, and I am not advocating that people just get sober and sit in a chair. But I *am* saying that one should not lose sight of the priority—which is *sobriety,* not goodness, not cosmic unity, not obedience to the will of a so-called higher power—it's sobriety itself. Sobriety is a priority, but it's not an obsession. It offers a kind of backdrop, so you can *have* a life, one you can make as meaningful as you can. If people want to just be, they can do that, too, and be sober; I have met such people. And I rejoice in their sobriety.

CORRECTING SOME
DANGEROUS MYTHS

The traditional psychologists say that you have to go back deep into your past and find out what happened between you and your Mommy and Daddy (or whomever), and then work through the unresolved feelings you have for them. Only by "getting in touch" with these emotions, the theory goes, can you feel okay.

Cognitive therapists, on the other hand, deal with "here and now" stuff. They say, "let's take a rational look at your problems and find out whether you're exaggerating them, or whether you are thinking in a distorted way." SOS takes the cognitive approach.

Let's look at an example: People often say of themselves, "I'm a total shit." Very few people are total shits. You may have behaved badly at a particular time, but you're not and never will be irredeemable. To take such an extreme view of yourself is unwarranted. As Albert Ellis, the father of cognitive therapy, has said, totally extreme statements are not productive. Why? *Because they are not true.* Another thing that's not true: the idea of an "alcoholic" or "addictive" personality. Problems in living are certainly *exacerbated* by chemical addiction, but they don't bring on "cellular thirst."

Some experts on alcoholism feel that alcoholics can "unlearn" drinking behaviors and thus modify their intake. This is a ludicrous idea. I wonder, do they plan eventually to apply this approach to cocaine and heroin users as well?

Even though an alcoholic can control his or her drinking for varying periods of time, what has he or she gained in the process? Writes one scientist, "Their situation was analogous to driving a car without a spare tire—disaster was usually only a matter of time."[4]

If an alcoholic chooses a life of sobriety, what has he or she *lost* in the process?

*   *   *

A number of years ago I stood by the hospital bed of a close friend. He was dead. He had been "only a heavy drinker," diagnosed as "nonalcoholic." Yet he died of alcohol-related deterioration. The doctors in attendance said that he "fell apart" physically. He was only forty-seven. I've known persons of all ages who have tried time after time to find a way to handle their "problem drinking." I can't think of a single case where sobriety would have brought them harm. I told you at the outset that I had a seven-month interruption in my seventeen years of consuming alcohol. That period of sobriety ended with a bizarre "celebration": I was "able to drink again." To "prove" it, I downed a fifth of premixed vodka martinis. When I related this to my therapist at the time, she agreed that "this, indeed, makes good sense."

Several years later, when I got sober again, I had a more difficult time of it. To wit: screaming and shaking and sweating and thinking that I was dying. My alcoholism had deepened profoundly, and I had abandoned my nonchalant attitude as well as my agreeable therapist. By so doing I abandoned the alcoholic's most persistant nemesis: *denial.*

Those seven months had merely been a "time out." Visions of future drinks were dancing in my head. I had had no program, no strategies for (or commitment to) my sobriety. Now I do.

In 1978, when I began my second period of sobriety, I was scared shitless. I have wanted to retain the positive essence of this "scared shitlessness" as a way of maintaining a healthy respect for my arrested condition. I wanted a life of sobriety this time, not dreams of future drinks. And I was willing to do whatever was required to achieve that.

As I mentioned earlier, during my first year of sobriety I questioned a number of sober alcoholics, searching for the common thread for their successes in maintaining a lasting sobriety. When I was about three years into my sobriety, I began to challenge some of the concepts of Alcoholics Anonymous, feeling that I stood alone in that endeavor. By the time I was sober for five years, I had compiled an extensive file of responses and, from four years ago to the present day, I've collected data from more than two thousand "secular sobrietists." Both from this research and from my own experience of recovery, I have put together a specific secular approach to achieving and maintaining long-term sobriety. I call it the "Sobriety

Priority." I wish to offer it here as *a* way (beware of anyone who offers *the* way) to achieve and maintain sobriety for life.

Unlike the program offered by AA, this secular approach does not require belief in a "higher power." Nor is it a "spiritual" or "twelve-step" program. And it's not a package deal. Achieving and maintaining sobriety is approached as a *separate issue,* not as part of a larger mystic/holistic plan, a plan that requires that you fear your very human imperfections. With the "Sobriety Priority," you accept the reality of the unfolding circumstances of your life; you know that you will on occasion always have painful or distressing feelings. You need not tread an eggshell-laden, straight-and-narrow pathway. Your sobriety, in this program, is protected cognitively as an untouchable, highly cherished, separate issue. Drinking alcohol or using other mind-altering drugs becomes a non-option.

No, I'm not recommending some break-all-the-rules lifestyle. (I do support one's right to self-determination, however.) I'm simply illustrating this point: By making sobriety itself one's baseline priority, you're protected from relapse. The indulgences and catastrophies of life may touch you, but they need never reach your sobriety.

Indeed, scientists have found that sociopathic persons can stay sober right along with the rest of us. According to one study, "eventual stable abstinence was not seen only among alcoholics with good premorbid adjustment. In the Core City sample, stable abstinence occurred most often in untreated and severely alcohol-dependent individuals. Sociopathic Core City alcoholics, . . . if anything, became abstinent younger and more frequently than did the sample's upper-middle-class college graduates selected for mental health."[5]

Our ideal, of course, is to grow, to *change for the better;*

the very act of staying sober facilitates and necessitates change at certain levels. But sobriety is the first and the mightiest improvement of one's life quest. Without that there's virtually no life to live, merely an existence garbled by buzzing, woozy dreams, progressively growing more meaningless with the natural progression of one's alcoholism, which is worsened still by the natural aging process.

Again, I want to emphasize that I am not condoning "scoundrelism." Most of us are, on occasion, only rascals. I am simply acknowledging the right of sober scoundrels to exist. This obviously offers real hope for the rest of us. Look, if those who are not too "tightly wrapped" can achieve and maintain sobriety as a separate issue, you can, too.

In short:

You can be a scoundrel—and be sober.

You can be a couch potato—and be sober.

Your brain can be brimming with ugly thoughts—and you can be sober.

You can be sober.

SOME MORE MYTHS

"Writers and artists are creative because they drink heavily."
Tom Dardis shows conclusively how wrong this myth is in his
recent book, *The Thirsty Muse: Alcohol and the American Writer*.
Dardis looks at four of this century's greatest writers, who were
also famous alcoholics: William Faulkner, Ernest Hemingway,
Eugene O'Neill, and F. Scott Fitzgerald. With the exception
of O'Neill, who was eventually able to quit drinking and maintain
sobriety, each author's ability to write grew more and more
impaired as his alcoholism progressed.

"You'll drink again if you don't 'come to believe' in a
'Higher Power,' a 'God as you understand Him.'" Not true.

"You'll drink again if you don't 'live' or 'work' the twelve-
step program to the best of your ability." Not true.

"You'll drink again if you don't attend lots of AA meetings."
Not true.

"You'll drink again if you don't 'pass it on'—i.e. 'carry the message' to other alcoholics." Not true.

"You'll drink again if you ever set out on your own. You need lifelong outside support." Not true.

O.K. Then why AA? Why SOS?

Religious/spiritual organizations tend to "hype" their members. Fear is a great motivator. They may say, "After all, your life was a wreck before you came here. You were obviously living it wrong." This is the pathway for the multitudes of the *faithful*. It is *one* way to acquire and maintain sobriety. Aside from sobriety, it is also the pathway or "leap of faith" for rock stars, politicians, and other assorted "sinners" to cast off the hedonism of their banal existences. But another option exists: the way of reason and compassion through free choice.

Sure, one can do one's "own thing" and eschew groups of any kind. And some do. Again, why AA? Because the support, warmth, love, and mutual sharing offered in a spiritual setting is a seductive and powerful phenomenon.

Why SOS? Because the support, warmth, love, and mutual sharing offered in a secular setting is a liberating and powerful phenomenon.

Throughout human history religious/spiritual movements have flourished, complete with holy writs, guru/saviors, "enforcement squads," and hordes of "the faithful," fearful of their own heretical free-thought processes. But animal urges are part of our humanity. Dominance and submissiveness are simply a continuation of our lizard leanings.

As human animals, we've got lots of choices. We can think, reason, and feel. Movements based on human reason and compassion have served in their particular time-frames. When new information emerges, secularists skeptically look it over, and, since life is an ongoing process, they choose as best they can, discarding and embracing as necessary.

Self-preservation and altruism are alive and well in both AA and SOS groups. True, one needn't practice altruism in a group setting, or at all for that matter. And self-preservation can be practiced in the comfort of one's own home. Of course, AA might counter that one loses out on the "spiritual dimension" without its group interaction.

As for SOS, one member recently expressed these thoughts: "Sure, I'm a secular person. I've been sober nine years, but I was never really comfortable in AA meetings. I know that I'm ultimately responsible for preserving my sobriety, but part of my continuing awareness process is the opportunity to share my experiences with other sober alcoholics here in these meetings. I don't often have the opportunity to share my 'sobriety stuff' with my colleagues or nonalcoholic friends. Frankly, they've got their own lives to live and their own interests. Some can't relate to alcoholism, and it's really not appropriate to share my thoughts and feelings related about sobriety with them, so I come here.

"SOS meetings are a tool I use in order to help maintain my awareness. I want to stay sober, and this is a part of that process for me. And I want to be there for others, especially newly sober people. I like this. I really enjoy being with you people and I look forward to these meetings."

The continuing growth of SOS is really up to us, its members. There is, after all, no carrot-on-a-stick motivation here. Unlike religious and other feelings-before-thought movements, SOS, as any rational approach, offers no magic quick fix. It does, however, offer an option, a viable alternative. You may keep your dignity, your individuality, and you need not check your mind at the door upon entering.

Welcome.

THE CYCLE OF ADDICTION

The *sobriety priority* approach for achieving and maintaining freedom from alcohol and other mind-altering drugs is a cognitive strategy. It can be applied, on a daily basis, as long as you live, to prevent relapse.

The sobriety priority approach respects the power of "nature" (genetic inheritance, progressive disease processes) and of "nurture" (learned habit, behaviors, and associations) by showing how to achieve the initial arrest of cellular addiction and stave off the chronic habits that result from this addiction.

The "cycle of addiction" contains three debilitating elements: *chemical need* (at the physiological cellular level), *learned habit* (chronic drinking/using behaviors and associations), and *denial* of both need and habit.

The Cycle of Addiction

The cycle of alcohol addiction usually develops over a period of years. Cycles have been found to be much shorter with other drugs, especially cocaine. In all cases, however, the addiction becomes "Priority One," a separate issue from everything else. And as it progresses, it begins to *negate* everything else.

THE CYCLE OF SOBRIETY

The cycle of addiction can be successfully replaced by another cycle: *the cycle of sobriety*. This cycle contains three essential elements: *acknowledgment* of one's addiction to alcohol or drugs (you may have euphemistically called it "a problem"); *acceptance* of one's disease/habit; and *prioritization* of sobriety as the primary issue in one's life.

The daily cognitive application of one's new "Priority One," the sobriety priority, *as a separate issue,* arrests the cycle of addiction. It frees the sober alcoholic/addict to experience "everything else," by teaching him or her to associate "everything else" with sobriety, not with drinking or using behaviors. The cycle of sobriety remains in place only so long as the sober alcoholic/addict cognitively chooses to continue to acknowledge the existence of his or her alcoholism and drug addiction.

This cannot be said too often: Your addiction can be "arrested," but you must acknowledge that you are still addicted.

This is your lifelong reality.

You should say something like the following every day: "My name is _____. I acknowledge that I am an alcoholic/addict. I accept that I cannot drink alcohol or use other mind-altering drugs, no matter what I may think, experience, feel. My sobriety is my first priority, and it is a separate issue from everything else in my life."

Another affirmation could go like this: "My name is _____. I am an alcoholic/addict. I cannot and do not drink or use, no matter what. My sobriety is my priority, and an issue separate from all else." Both versions express acknowledgment, acceptance, and prioritization.

The sobriety priority, applied daily, gradually weakens booze and drug associations, halting the cycle of addiction, allowing time for new associations to form as one experiences his or her life without addictive chemicals. As one continues to "make peace" with the facts regarding his or her arrested addiction— that is, as one continues to recognize alcohol and drugs as a *non*-option—one comes *to prefer* a sober lifestyle; one longs to preserve it, to respect one's arrested chemical addiction, to protect one's sober life.

ACKNOWLEDGMENT

Drinking stopped "working" for me. The price for my pleasure-center fix became too high. I glimpsed my mortality in a real blood-and-guts, finite way. My romanticized dream-views fell apart. It was then that I acknowledged that my Priority One had become drinking alcohol. I accepted that I could not stop drinking once I started. It then occurred to me that if I stopped and "stayed stopped," no matter what came my way, it would probably be better than my then current life situation. And it was.

Through this acknowledgment and acceptance of my habit/disease, I began to desire to protect and maintain my sobriety, my *new* Priority One. I wanted continued relief from the intense pain of active alcoholism. I wanted freedom from the bondage of my cycle of addiction.

Today, I doubt that any external entity or "higher power," natural or supernatural, can crawl inside of me to keep me sober. I take responsibility for my own sobriety. I respect my arrested habit/disease. As I continue to stay sober, I think well of myself for my achievement. The very act of staying sober gives me self-esteem. Every day I credit myself for my continuing sobriety.

I'm never complacent. Complacency is deadly. A case in point: A thirty-five-year sober alcoholic, in his seventies, tells of an alcoholic who had been sober for thirty-four years (also in his seventies) who began drinking again, and who died soon after as a result of his drinking. My friend's comment was poignant: "Joe simply forgot that he couldn't drink."

That is a common phenomenon, especially in early sobriety. It often occurs after several months, when many alcoholics turn their attention away from their need to prioritize sobriety. They feel great. And their lives *are* much better. So they tell themselves, "Who needs this shit?" Then they drink again . . . and reinstate their cycle of addiction. "Hey, I'm better" might be a happy thought—but it's dangerous to confuse that thought with, "Hey, I'm *cured*," which is *never* true. I know this fact's not delightful to ponder. But it is only by pondering it that you will ever discover delight again. Getting real about one's addiction can be very difficult, but it yields tremendous return.

*   *   *

Recently I spoke with an alcoholic who, by his own admission, is dying. Like so many alcoholics/addicts, he views his life in a surreal way. His real focus is on satisfying his intense cellular pleasure-need. His chronic habit is firmly fixed. And his disease has nearly progressed to its final stages. I hope that he will glimpse at least a sliver of his mortality soon. This flash could disturb his twenty years of denial and allow him to begin his recovery. One must acknowledge alcoholism/addiction as one's here-and-now reality, in order to begin one's recovery.

ACCEPTANCE

Who among us really wants to accept that he or she has a severe problem, a handicap, a disease? Does a combat vet gleefully accept that he no longer has legs?

But acceptance is necessary to recovery. One has first to acknowledge, then accept facts that can no longer be denied. Denial can go on for years, and many persons die while in the process.

When the combat vet awakes each morning, he experiences the fact that he no longer has legs. Not so with alcoholics/addicts. Those of us who are sober alcoholics and addicts must reacknowledge and reaccept our arrested addictions every day. We have no motorized wheelchair gleaming in a bedroom corner to remind us to acknowledge and accept. Our reminder must be a mental, cognitive thing: "I acknowledge that I am an alcoholic. I accept that, because of my genetic predisposition to alcoholism, and my frontal-lobe recordings of past drinking behaviors, I cannot drink (or use) no matter what."

Some of us go through a brief period of mourning. We seem to have lost "old friends" in quitting alcohol and other drugs. The phenomenon, as far as I am concerned, is similar to that of hostages coming to identify with their terrorist captors. Called "the Stockholm Syndrome," it's normal for some—but of course it's completely irrational. In time, one comes to prefer a life of freedom, of sobriety, and that joyous realization is a pleasure to contemplate.

PRIORITIZATION AS A SEPARATE ISSUE

If one has acknowledged and accepted the reality of one's alcoholism or drug addiction, if one has really stopped denying his or her addiction, doesn't prioritizing sobriety as "numero uno" make sense?

That's the big difference between this approach and the twelve-step package deal. Other programs connect recovery to "spiritual" or emotional "growth," or to becoming a purer, more ethical person. Becoming a better person *is* wonderful—of course it is. But it does not necessarily have anything to do with becoming sober. Similarly, you didn't become an addict because you were scum; the "alcoholic personality" conception of addiction has fostered moralism, not progress; consequently, it has promoted not empowerment but low self-esteem.

There is another way. Simply put, cognitively prioritizing your sobriety means:

1. You choose to value that which affords you a life.

2. Your sobriety is an *untouchable*, separate issue. Drinking is not an option for you, because you are an alcoholic, i.e., you cannot drink with impunity; you cannot drink *and get away with it.*

3. As long as you continue to restate this commitment to yourself daily, thus acknowledging and accepting who you are, you're set free to experience everything else.

"Everything else" means that you can get angry, anxious, fearful, joyous, sad, thrilled, nervous, stressed, bored, jealous, intimate, and happy—experience the full gamut of your emotions—without fearing (as other programs suggest) that you are in a "relapse mode," or that you're on a "dry drunk." Connecting sobriety to necessary emotional states is risky business. Connecting it to the daily realization that you simply can't drink makes a lot more sense. This approach fits the evidence; it's a lot less confusing; and it *works.*

"Everything else" also means you can be an atheist, a believer, a rascal, a pauper, a king, a democrat, republican, libertarian, fascist, socialist, or combinations of any of the above, and *still stay sober.* The church of circumstances is separate from the state of your sobriety.

Sobriety as a separate issue means that you can stay sober and then choose your very own "quality of life program." If you march to the sound of a different drummer, you can do so—soberly.

There is so much diversity on this planet. We can deny it, but it won't go away. I suggest that as sober alcoholics/ addicts we accept diversity, then prioritize our own individual sobriety, allowing others the freedom to live their own lives, at their own pace, in their own style, as long as they don't infringe on our rights to do likewise.

NEW ASSOCIATIONS

Emotional support and the understanding of others is vital in the early stages of sobriety. Listening to others describe how they dealt with feelings and situations of stress and pain when *they* were newly sober is extremely helpful. Since most everything is a "reason to drink" for the chronic addict, one must go through daily life in order to make it through daily life sober. The feeling of self-esteem comes immediately *if* we credit *ourselves* for our new sobriety daily.

Nonaddicts and nonalcoholics may or may not applaud us. *We* applaud each other. We must keep our objectivity fresh, our exuberance for sobriety alive, or we will relapse and the fall will be harder.

We tend to live our lives in twenty-four hour periods. So, as each new day passes, we brush our teeth, comb our hair, succeed, fail, laugh, cry, argue, learn, experience setbacks, feel pain, think dark thoughts, regret losses, pity ourselves, accept ourselves, dislike ourselves, and experience highs and lows *in sobriety*. And in sobriety, this all becomes new, as if done for the first time. Every day is a victory.

*   *   *

When we ingest drugs, we tamper with our delicate neurological balance. Many times this alteration seems to be of minimal consequence, as in the case of social drinkers. Others can develop addictions, and find their lives consumed. An addiction to alcohol or drugs takes on a life of its own, and the person addicted literally becomes secondary, a slave, as the feeding of one's "needy cells" becomes the addicted person's number one priority.

Scientists say that *Homo sapiens* is genetically programmed to be a creature of habit. When we learn things, we in a sense "own" them. Behavior is imprinted onto our brains, for "call-up," when related associations come along. For alcoholics and addicts, drinking and using tends to be associated with just about everything.

In my drinking days, for example, I associated booze with butterfly wings, turkey legs, neon signs, world peace, good times, bad times, creativity, pathos, inhaling, exhaling, making dinner, making love—just about everything. My hand-to-glass-to-bottle (to-hell-with-the-glass)-to-mouth reflexes would operate "faster than your neurotransmitters could fire," as one friend said to me.

However, habits can be changed cognitively, and associations can be weakened.

But it's harder for *any* human being to practice cognition when he or she is even moderately under the influence of a mind-altering drug (including alcohol), because his or her reasoning processes are in an altered state, allowing the primitive, older brain processes to hold forth. To attempt to modify drinking behavior in one who has previously experienced "problem drinking" is a risky proposition, and potentially dangerous. Dangerous changes to deadly when one's drinking history has been heavy, chronic, and long-term.

When viewing alcoholism from the cellular-addictive standpoint, two points also emerge:

(1) Once the cells are freed (initially by medical detoxification, and then by a day-by-day program of abstinence) from the chemical to which they are predisposed to be addicted, it then becomes crucial to keep these cells away from the addictive chemicals.

(2) If the drugs are reingested, the cells will be "waiting" for their chemical fix in human brains and bodies that cannot safely process alcohol. The original need (for alcohol transmogrified into "heroin") is once again fired up. Cellular need, primitive need, does not request compliance—it demands it.

COGNITIVE DISTORTIONS

As one's time in sobriety lengthens, one must still continue one's daily focus on sobriety as a separate issue in order to continue one's freedom from alcohol and drugs. Even if one assumes a minimally adventurous role in life (due to one's circumstances, choices, or a combination of the two), one can remain sober with continued acknowledgment, acceptance, and prioritization of sobriety as one's primary issue.

I know a woman who has achieved about fifteen years of non-continuous sobriety. Her sobriety, she says, is "no big deal." She seems perpetually miserable. During these fifteen years she has relapsed on numerous occasions, but managed, fortunately, to return to sobriety each time. She sees her sobriety as an unpleasant *task*, not potentially her finest achievement. She really hasn't accepted the fact that she is an alcoholic. Denial persists, and rears its ugly head periodically, as her alcohol-related resentments build to a life-threatening crescendo, and explode into the inevitable relapse: "Why can't I be like everyone else? Why can't I control and enjoy my drinking? Life isn't fair. Goddamn it, *I deserve more*. This planet sucks. It's all a cosmic joke anyhow—so, what the hell, break out the booze if that's all there is!"

Cognitive distortions abound in this person's mind. If she really acknowledged, accepted, and prioritized her sobriety as her primary achievement in life, her nihilism would weaken, her denial would crumble, and the value of her accomplishment in sobriety would spill over into all of her life, lifting her depression and the skewed perceptions that go along with it. Cognitive distortions destroy; cognitive sobriety nurtures. She needn't have a "Jesus injection" or travel to the Andes for "spiritual enlightenment." She could lighten up by realizing, "Your feelings are not facts! In fact, your feelings, per se, don't even count—except as a mirror of the way you are thinking. If your perceptions make no sense, the feelings they create will be as absurd as the images reflected in the trick mirrors at an amusement park. But these abnormal emotions *feel* just as valid and realistic as the genuine feelings created by undistorted thoughts, so you automatically attribute truth to them. . . . "[7] This good advice comes from David D. Burns, M.D., author of *Feeling Good: The New Mood Therapy*. Dr. Burns offers a table of "Definitions of Cognitive Distortions":

1. ALL-OR-NOTHING THINKING: You see things in black-and-white categories. If your performance falls short of perfect, you see yourself as a total failure.

pas de refuser la fécondité mais de faire naître en exerçant une régulation, c'est-à-dire en mettant en œuvre, de façon moralement responsable, le pouvoir de maîtrise sur lui-même que Dieu a confié à l'être humain.

2. *Une pratique jamais anodine* contraception

L'idéologie sociale dominante voudrait faire croire que la pratique de la régulation des naissances est anodine : à la limite, il ne serait pas plus impliquant pour une femme d'absorber une pilule contraceptive que de boire un verre d'eau et les malaises ressentis dans le couple par la mise en œuvre de la contraception ne seraient que l'effet de tabous judéo-chrétiens mal dépassés. Une telle façon de penser ne résiste pas à une analyse scientifique sérieuse. Il faut affirmer que la régulation des naissances est toujours une pratique qui implique en profondeur les personnalités.

En premier lieu, les répercussions *physiologiques* de certaines méthodes contraceptives dites modernes ne sont pas toujours négligeables [10]. C'est bien pourquoi, la prise de contraceptifs chimiques doit se faire sous contrôle médical.

En second lieu, les *psychismes* des personnes qui mettent en œuvre la régulation des naissances sont profondément mobilisés. Utiliser une méthode contraceptive c'est en effet toujours être amené à une série de prises de position face à des réalités très importantes de la vie : le rapport à la sexualité et au plaisir, la relation au conjoint et aux enfants déjà nés, la façon de se situer comme femme ou homme dans la société, le désir d'être parent, le droit de regard de la médecine sur la vie privée, les positions éthiques de l'Eglise ou de l'entourage... On devine dès lors que toutes ces prises de positions ne sont pas sans répercussions, parfois considérables, sur les conjoints. D'autant plus que les recherches récentes de la psychanalyse font comprendre que l'*inconscient* est particulièrement actif dans la pratique de la régulation. La façon

---

10. Cf. *Laënnec*, hiver 1980-1981, la contraception : après vingt ans de pratique.

LA RÉGULATION DES NAISSANCES

Eléments d'une réflexion éthique [8]

La pratique de la contraception dans nos sociétés occidentales est devenue chose banale pour beaucoup d'hommes et de femmes. Si banale que pour de nombreux chrétiens, l'utilisation d'une méthode contraceptive a cessé d'être un problème moral pour devenir purement et simplement un problème technique. Ce qui importe c'est de trouver la méthode la plus efficace et la plus satisfaisante d'un point de vue médical et psychologique. La dimension éthique de la conduite contraceptive est alors occultée, tant et si bien que les plaidoyers du pape en faveur des méthodes naturelles [9] apparaissent à beaucoup comme un combat d'arrière-garde. Or il me semble que cet effacement de la réflexion éthique est grave car il risque de soumettre les chrétiens et tous les membres de notre société à la pression subreptice d'idéologies bien peu conformes à la vérité évangélique. Je me contenterai ici, au risque de paraître simplificateur, d'énoncer quelques convictions anthropologiques et quelques repères éthiques à ne pas négliger sous peine de rendre déshumanisante la pratique contraceptive.

1. Mieux vaut parler de régulation des naissances

Les questions de vocabulaire ne sont jamais secondaires, car les mots sont chargés d'anthropologie. C'est pourquoi je pense qu'il faut employer l'expression «régulation des naissances» de préférence à celle de «contraception». Ce dernier terme connote trop la seule opération technique par laquelle on empêche la fécondation de se réaliser. Au contraire, l'expression «régulation des naissances» implique d'emblée une dimension éthique. Elle fait comprendre qu'il ne s'agit

---

8. Revue *Choisir,* mai 1982.
9. Jean-Paul II, *Familiaris consortio* n° 31-34 in *Doc. Cath.,* 3-1-82.

2. OVERGENERALIZATION: You see a single negative event as a never-ending pattern of defeat.

3. MENTAL FILTER: You pick out a single negative detail and dwell on it exclusively so that your vision of all reality becomes darkened, like the drop of ink that discolors the entire beaker of water.

4. DISQUALIFYING THE POSITIVE: You reject positive experiences by insisting they "don't count" for some reason or other. In this way you can maintain a negative belief that is contradicted by your everyday experiences.

5. JUMPING TO CONCLUSIONS: You make a negative interpretation even though there are no definite facts that convincingly support your conclusion.

> a. *Mind Reading.* You arbitrarily conclude that someone is reacting negatively to you, and you don't bother to check this out.

> b. *The Fortune Teller Error.* You think that things will turn out badly, and you feel convinced that your prediction is an already-established fact.

6. MAGNIFICATION (CATASTROPHIZING) OR MINIMIZATION: You exaggerate the importance of things (such as your goof-up or someone else's achievement), or you inappropriately shrink things until they appear tiny (your own desirable qualities or the other fellow's imperfections). This is also called the "binocular trick."

7. EMOTIONAL REASONING: You assume that your negative emotions necessarily reflect the way things really are: "I feel it, therefore it must be true."

8. "SHOULD" STATEMENTS: You try to motivate yourself with "shoulds'" and "shouldn'ts," as if you had to be whipped and punished before you could be expected to do anything. "Musts" and "oughts" are also offenders. The emotional consequence is guilt. When you direct "should" statements toward others, you feel anger, frustration, and resentment.

9. LABELING AND MISLABELING: This is an extreme form of overgeneralization. Instead of describing your error, you attach a negative label to yourself. "I'm a *loser*." When someone else's behavior rubs you the wrong way, you attach a negative label to him: "He's a goddam louse." Mislabeling involves describing an event with language that is highly colored and emotionally loaded.

10. PERSONALIZATION: You see yourself as the cause of some negative external event which in fact you were not primarily responsible for.

"CALLING UP" TECHNIQUES

Let's say you've been off booze for several months, or years. You don't feel tempted to walk into the corner bar. When something goes wrong at the office, or in the bedroom, you don't yearn to go out and buy alcohol. You feel you've kicked it.

You feel "normal." Having beaten back alcoholism, you can return to normal drinking.

Wrong.

You are an alcoholic for life. Accept that. You can be confident that you will keep your sobriety, but you can never be complacent.

How does one avoid such complacency? By "calling up" vivid images of yourself-as-active-alcoholic. What these images do is bring you back to acknowledgment and acceptance of your alcoholism, and to reprioritization of your sobriety.

By calling it up (but not wallowing in it), you remember alcohol's true, inescapable effect on you.

I call up the image of myself waking up in my own vomit. I see it vividly, truthfully—and briefly. (There's no need to dwell on it or "hype it up.") And I remember, forcefully, that particular humiliation, one of many I had as an alcoholic. And I see that it could become real again. Other sober alcoholics "call up" car wrecks. A fellow in one SOS group, who has five years sobriety, recently told his group that he felt he was becoming complacent. So he called up an image of himself driving his car, drunk, his little boy on the front seat—his little boy, who had innocently and lovingly placed all his trust in his big strong Daddy. But he was drunk. He didn't get into a car wreck, he didn't kill his son; but he easily could have, and in calling up that possibility, he shudders, and he remembers, and gone is that complacency, that most dangerous frame of mind.

Other people recall the night they attended a very important event, like a graduation, at which they gravely embarrassed themselves in front of the people they loved most. One woman calls up the time she went to a banquet honoring her husband. She got drunk, fell down on the salad, and then onto the floor. You might say that this scene has comical aspects. You might say, "That's not really dramatic compared to what *I* did, or to what I have heard." But calling up that image works for her, because that was the moment she realized: *I have got to do something about this—this is not a real life. Look at what I did to my husband! He's a good guy—and I mortified him in front of his colleagues.*

A man I know from SOS calls up those times he used to wake up in the park. Here was a guy who wasn't a homeless wino; he had a job—he was "functioning," as many alcoholics do. But he would go out and get so drunk he would wander out in a park near where he lived and kibitz with the derelicts there. He could have been killed or mugged or maimed. He would wake up the next day: "My God, what have I done?" So he remembers . . . *"This,"* he says, "is where drinking used to take me: disoriented in the wide-open morning, the dew on the grass, the stink in my mouth." And the shame. And, finally, the decision not to drink anymore. Calling up the image reinforces his resolve.

Then there are those who call up the time when they went to bed with somebody they wish they hadn't. That's a very common one, and quite effective, as you might imagine.

But just about any unpleasant thing you wouldn't do while sober is a good call-up—whatever has meaning, whatever's *your* story.

Your *old* story.

DRINK DREAMS

Have you been troubled by the fact that you have "drink dreams"? Relax. This phenomenon is common to all sober alcoholics. These dreams will come and go.

Remember when you dreamed of a long-deceased loved one being alive? When you woke up, remember how overwhelmed you were by feelings of grief? Well, consider this: When you have troubling "drink dreams," and you awaken to find that it was only a dream, you feel relieved and exhilarated, right? Quite a difference from the sad thoughts and feelings that arise from your "dead loved one" dream.

THE PANIC ATTACK

I have often been asked, "What do I do when I get a panic attack? I always used to reach for a drink to calm me down."

That's the beauty of the sobriety-priority program. You no longer have to fear that bad experiences are going to "drive you to drink." They can make you feel like hiding under a table, or wishing that you were on another planet. But, when you have prioritized sobriety as a separate issue from everything else, you no longer make any specific state of mind or affairs a *condition* of sobriety.

Indeed, I accept that I am *not* always going to handle my problems in a perfect way. Just like most folks, we stew in our own juices from time to time.

Many of us have found that the best way to handle a panic attack is to sit down and go over the thing rationally: Am I making a mountain out of a molehill? Am I giving myself over to distorted thoughts? But we don't even think of drinking, because we consider that a non-option. No matter how heavy-duty a problem seems, it's not the end of the world. If I made a mess of something, if I broke a commitment, I can try to do better next time; I can work on it. But I also realize there will *always* be things that won't be the way I want them to be. But whatever else, I still have my sobriety.

WHERE YOU CAN GO

I am a citizen of the world, and I love to travel. Some people think, however, that sober alcoholics should stay away from "slippery" places. When I became sober, I had to continue going to cocktail parties; business required it. I just realized who I was—and I felt *protected*. No environment can make me feel antsy. I don't worry about temptation. Drinking is a non-option for me if I want to stay alive. That is a fact. If my neighbor is having a martini or two, that's his business; it has nothing to do with me.

I feel comfortable with people who drink. But I also feel bored around people who are drunk, or who are getting drunk, because they tend to repeat themselves. If I go with friends to a bar or nightclub, it is to enjoy the comraderie of my friends or the fun of the show; the drinking aspect just has no interest for me.

In other words, you are free to go anywhere—with anyone. No place, no person determines your sobriety for you. It's you (and only you) who can do that.

DRUG THERAPIES

This sober alcoholic was trying to help. "Well Jim, it looks like we might be putting you on the breakfast of champions"—i.e., antabuse.

When he said that, I thought, "I must be really bad off if this guy is trying to prod me to take that drug, and in such a humorous way, instead of simply saying, 'Jim, you're dying, so let's try this.'" I was almost humiliated by his kindness, by the idea that I would have to take antabuse to stay sober. "I must be one of the real *cases*," I thought.

Well, what about antabuse? Doctors sometimes prescribe antabuse to alcoholics in order to get them to stop drinking. The way it works is simple: If you take a drink while you are on antabuse, you get violently ill. The drug is not meant to be used forever, and it has been known to cause psychotic reactions in some people who've stayed on it too long. In the earliest stage of sobriety, however, it has helped some people.

I used it when I was still denying my alcoholism, for dieting purposes. I knew that alcohol had all these empty calories. My doctor put me on antabuse. (You should *never* use this drug without consulting a doctor.) Sometimes the doctor will stand by you to make sure you take it. But you can't live in a pen (or clinic) where people are following you around. It is not the permanent answer, because eventually you are going to have to stay sober yourself.

What about the use of other drugs as a way of getting off of alcohol?

Librium, for example, is sometimes prescribed for detoxification, to aid those alcoholics who might otherwise have seizures or the DTs. This and other drugs are used so that alcoholics are brought down in such a way that they won't be harmed.

Drugs are sometimes prescribed by doctors *after* the detoxification phase as well, for cases of what has been called the "dual diagnosis." A dual diagnosis is when in addition to alcoholism the patient suffers from some other condition—manic depression, for example—which might require medication.

Not all doctors, unfortunately, understand that alcoholics require special attention when receiving prescription medication.

Doctors have to make sure that they aren't prescribing medication that gets the sober alcoholic "high."

SOME *GOOD* MIND GAMES

Here are some sobriety mind games. Let's get extreme. Suppose there is a nuclear holocaust. If I happen to survive the bombs, I picture myself making myself useful, searching for meaning even in the midst of these circumstances. I would do whatever I could to help care for the wounded; I would console survivors and be a part of whatever life activities remain. Even in a post-apocalyptic world, "breaking out the booze" wouldn't interest me. As a sober alcoholic, no reason in our natural universe exists for me to have a drink.

I am free to experience life in the real world. Since my perception of at least one part of me is correct—that I am a sober alcoholic—then I've got all kinds of other things to think about, to feel, and to do. There's lots in life besides drinking or using. From this point I can proceed. More and more I find that my perspective begins to match my perceptions in the other areas of my life as well.

Want to get high? Get physical! Feel the daily improvement in your health, your muscle tone. Go for a brisk walk in walking shoes or strip down to the raw in the privacy of your own place. Flip on the radio or stereo, and do some aerobics. Jump and dance around to your favorite upbeat music.

Want to lower your anxiety level and blood pressure, and feel loved and needed in the process? Invite a nonhuman companion into your home. Apartment dwellers faced with "no pets allowed" regulations can usually get around this restriction (which usually translates to "no dogs or cats") by bringing home a gerbil, bird, turtle, or fish.

Feeling especially sad, unloved, long-suffering, rejected, or put upon at the moment? The following mind game can help when your emotions are especially hurt or raw: Picture a galley slave or a brutalized handmaiden from our ancient past. See and feel his or her suffering. Did he or she, as have legions of human beings, suffer unjustly? Feel love and compassion for this human suffering; reach out to these ancient folks in your mind. Life is not fair; it simply unfolds. But *we* can be fair; *we* can reach out to each other. We are, at times, not loved. We are, at times, treated unfairly. You can identify with our ancient brothers and sisters. Can you imagine that you would love them if they were here? Can you imagine that they would also acknowledge your suffering and return your loving-kindness?

There are many people throughout history you can reach out to in your mind, for mutual support when immediate support is not available. Logically, truthfully, and factually you can see that someone, somewhere, would have reached back to you. Feel this healing, comforting warmth; hug yourself. We are never truly alone in the timelessness of our imaginations. You have a common bond with all humanity. In this, your moment of sorrow, draw strength and consolation, for you can be loved always in your own mind. Yes, you are worthy of love. Feel your own love now, for yourself, and for all those gentle people. Screw the scoundrels of the world! You have a right to be, to exist. You are here. Claim your right, now. Feel your power, your individual strength and warmth surging through every cell in your body, with every breath.

When I feel *especially* raw, I, as a sober alcoholic, see and feel this truth: "IF NOTHING ELSE, I STILL HAVE MY SOBRIETY."

When we're feeling down, many times our emotions are derived from distorted thoughts, skewed perspectives. Of course we feel appropriately sad from loss; but for the most part, feelings from correct perspectives have limits. They don't drag on and on. In my sobriety I have not once experienced the black blacks, those low lows, that I did in my drinking days. For in spite of everything else, I really do *still have my sobriety*. In that happy truth, I can find at least one accurate perspective, which frees me to observe the world objectively in the other areas of my life.

FROM THERE TO HERE

Now that you are (and continue to be) "off the juice and on the loose," the world is your oyster. Your dreary drinking is history. Colors are brighter, sounds are sharper, and real life is *realer*. Aren't you grateful that life no longer passes you by, drifting away on a sodden sea of alcohol, with syringes, needles, bottles of pills and potions, envelopes of white powder smeared with droplets of blood, and rolled reefers drifting by?

May I be one of the first to congratulate you in your sobriety. As a fellow sober alcoholic, let me heartily welcome you to real life.

When we are newly sober, some of us have our families and friends still in place, our jobs intact. Some of us do not. In either case, we start anew, rebuilding our damaged relationships, reshaping our careers as best we can, sober.

*   *   *

A while back I ran into a six-year sober alcoholic in another town. He now works with troubled teenagers, counseling them regarding their drug and alcohol addictions. While we were walking back to our cars after a long talk in a nearby coffeeshop, he showed some sights to me.

"This is where I used to pick up cocaine." He pointed to an area in a shopping mall across the street. "And this is where I made the exchanges out of the trunk of my car years ago." Only as I was about to drive away did he tell me this: "Years ago, just before I stopped drinking and using and dealing drugs, I was driving drunk one night and lost control of my car, crashing into the side of a frame house, killing a mother who was holding her baby." How'd you like to deal with that one? This man must live with this knowledge every day. Compared to him, most of us have lucked out. I know *I* lucked out. I drove and drank on numerous occasions, but I never killed anyone. Moreover, I never got into cocaine, pills, or other drugs— basically because the opportunity never presented itself. But many people come into sobriety poly-addicted. Many sold drugs or even their bodies in order to support their habits. Sure, alcohol is legal and accessible, but that doesn't make booze better than illegal drugs. I was a "functioning drunk." I maintained a job, and would walk into any liquor store of my choosing to support my habit/disease. But the "legality" of my drug did not make me better than any other addict.

*   *   *

Once upon a time, an inebriated gynecologist entered his operating room and began a routine operation he felt he could "almost do blindfolded." After removing an ovarian cyst, he mumbled, "here's one I missed," and he proceeded to cut out the patient's bladder. Soon thereafter, when the "mistake" was discovered, the head of urology intervened, attempting to build a new bladder for the patient from her lower intestine. As a consequence of this, she became a hemiplegic; later she suffered a stroke.

Impaired professionals make their rounds daily, insert needles, file briefs, rev up jet engines for overseas flights, and shred top-secret government documents while their heads reel, their noses bleed, and their vision blurs.

Meanwhile, back in the alcoholism/addiction field, massive grants continue to fund some alcoholism professionals who teach that moderation is the answer. These people think that sobriety is "too extreme" for some to achieve.

Prohibition is not the solution here, but, in my view, neither are half-assed treatments that propose to correct alcoholism by advocating "controlled drinking" rather than sobriety. It's hard. Booze flows and drugs flourish in our society. But alcoholics and addicts have a viable choice—the option of sobriety. I have never witnessed a painted corpse, dead from an overdose, that was particularly romantic. And I've never seen a spiritual incantation resurrect a stiff. Happily, I have witnessed many persons restored to real life, via sobriety. The intoxicants are there. The freedom is here.

The choice is ours.

OTHER VOICES

THE MEDIA

Newspapers, magazines, radio, and television have helped spread the message about the new secular alternative to AA. Even the *Grapevine*, the official voice of Alcoholics Anonymous, recently ran an article on SOS. The Council for Democratic and Secular Humanism (CODESH) has continued to be very supportive, publishing our national newsletter and helping to spread the word by mentioning SOS in each issue of its *Free Inquiry* magazines. Over fifty radio and television shows have covered "the SOS story."

SOS has received favorable coverage in diverse publications, including *Playboy, Glamour, The World, Changes (For and About Adult Children), East/West, The Utne Reader, The U.S. Journal of Drug and Alcohol Dependence, Monday Morning Report, The Substance Abuse Report, The Secular Humanist Bulletin, Freethought Today, The American Rationalist,* the *Los Angeles Times,* the *San Francisco Chronicle, Professional Counselor, Sober Times,* the *Buffalo News,* the *Detroit*

News, The Associated Press, *Tonawanda News,* the *Patriot Ledger,*
The Humanist, the *Chattanooga Times,* the *Milwaukee Journal,* the
Tolucan, SAGE (Human Resources Abstracts), the *Sunday Oregonian,*
the *Californian, The Foothill Ledger,* and numerous other publications. Abroad, SOS coverage has appeared in England's
Manchester Guardian and Australia's *The Age,* as well as publications
in Canada and the Netherlands.

Michael Robertson's *San Francisco Chronicle* story, published
on May 25, 1988, is representative:

Sobriety Without the Hand of God

Eight people sit around a rectangular table and talk. Their faces
are unremarkable, the sort of cross-section you'd find in any
place where strangers chance to meet. They could be here to
learn flower arranging or they might be planning to stop the
nearest war.

As it happens they are there because they are afraid of
dying one drink at a time. The routine is familiar: "My name
is _____ and I am an alcoholic"—the signature of a
typical Alcoholics Anonymous meeting.

But this is not AA. None of these recovering alcoholics
believes in God or any of the more comfortable euphemisms
for God, and that disbelief has made them uncomfortable with
AA's emphasis on a "higher power" to whom alcoholics must
surrender their lives.

Everyone talks. Everyone acknowledges his or her
alcoholism. A few also explain their secular humanism or free-
thinking or atheism.

Cathy, who is in her 40s, an unemployed social worker
and political activist, shares the moment of her great
disillusionment, when, thirty years ago, she saw a black man

refused medical treatment because of his race. She watched
him die.

"If that was God's will," she says, "no, thanks."

The group is the only Bay Area chapter of Secular
Organizations for Sobriety [there are now several], a grass-roots
movement committed to offering an alternative to an emphasis
on "spiritual steps" as the source of lasting sobriety.

Most of the 15 or so members tell the same story. AA
helped bring them back from alcohol and/or drugs. But their
respect and gratitude are in an uneasy balance with their
intellectual discomfort with certain aspects of AA.

Rich may be typical. A former college teacher with a Ph.D.
in the social sciences, he has been sober for six years. He helped
establish an atheists/agnostics meeting in San Francisco AA "to
meet my own needs. It was not met with resistance but with
discomfort. They wonder what goes on there."

He continues to attend general AA meetings, to step in
and let newcomers know you don't have to believe in God
to benefit.

He recalls his first AA meeting. He was befriended by
someone "who had combined free-thinking and sobriety for 32
years. (The lesson was) take what you can use and leave the
rest. That's how I stayed in the program, remembering that
this guy did it. That's why I will go back. I have many friends,
and I need to help people coming in. Who knows how many
walk in—and walk out.

"Sometimes at AA I have to grit my teeth. To stay sober
I wasn't going to convert to the Judeo-Christian tradition. They'd
say 'How can you stay sober without prayer?' "

A thoughtful man, he pauses. "We want the best of AA,
the good things."

Others express their differences more emphatically.

Janis, an attractive woman in her late 30s who operates her own bookkeeping business, recalls the days she was an AA "star," told that she was one of those people "chosen" by God for alcoholism, so that she could come out the other side stronger and better.

When she came into AA in 1980, "I plugged into the 'Higher Power' concept. I developed my own concept of 'The Force,' of universal human intelligence, something really foggy . . . "

Then "bad stuff" began happening to her, and "this nebulous higher power just wasn't there."

"I felt abandoned, lied to. The propaganda had me feeling I was one of the chosen, a sober alcoholic. I had been told that He—there's a lot of "Him" and not too much "Her" in AA—would never give me anything I couldn't handle. I couldn't handle what happened to me. I started drinking again. I underwent hard-won changes in my belief system. I put off going back to AA for over a year because I knew I would have trouble with the belief system."

Janis says many aspects of AA are valuable, particularly the power of group support and the emphasis on confronting your vulnerability as a non-drinking alcoholic. She thinks those forces will operate without the God talk.

"Faith is not the monopoly of theists. We have faith in ourselves and we have faith in each other."

The El Cerrito SOS had its first meeting three months ago. Members hope to see SOS programs accepted by courts and health professionals as a legitimate alternative to AA. If there are 10 million to 15 million alcoholics in the country and if AA reaches only 1 or 2 million, there is room for alternative approaches.

"This is an opportunity for AA," Janis says. "It's the first time they've been challenged. Though it is not our purpose to challenge."

That's the contradiction of SOS, of course. The founding members know that what they are doing will be interpreted as criticism of AA, and that concerns them, since a little theism does not seem too high a price to pay for saving lives.

But they all had come to feel intellectually dishonest.

"The problem is the religious content of AA," says Michael, a Berkeley sign-shop foreman. "It's not the emphasis on sobriety or anonymity. For those who only pay lip service to the idea of a higher power, (SOS) is the group. I was always having to do a mental translation, and I got tired of it . . . "

One is struck by the optimism of the SOS members. They think you can stay sober without putting the responsibility for your life on God or sin or Satan. They think accepting responsibility is what every recovering alcoholic in AA is really doing. No one gets up at an AA meeting and says, "My name is Bob, and God made me an alcoholic."

The group consensus: AA is fine if you get past the "Ultimate Authority" concept.

"That's a big if," Cathy says. "But our point is that 'secular' means 'without religious connotations or overtones.' We're here to stay sober . . . "

*   *   *

Getting media attention has not been too difficult. After all, SOS touches on two currently hot topics: addiction and religion. What we really gain is more than copy: We get the word out to other alcoholics, as well as to professional alcohol-recovery counselors and administrators. We can save more lives.

Traveling the country has given me a wonderful opportunity to meet other secular sobrietists. They have shared with me their ideas regarding the shape and scope of the SOS movement that they have worked hard to bring into being.

Reception of the SOS movement has been enthusiastic, but there have certainly been some thorns among the roses. On two occasions, chemical-dependency professionals allied with a major hospital chain invited representatives of SOS to come in to set up alternative meetings. Both times the "Twelve-Steppers" pressured their more open-minded colleagues to abort the new SOS meetings before they began. During one of the planning meetings, as members of SOS faced a committee of twenty alcoholism professionals, the program director asked, "What does spirituality mean to you people?"

One of the SOS members replied, "I really can't relate to that word. I'm happy to be sober and to be participating in life's adventure, with all its opportunities, challenges, and uncertainties. If you're referring to the 'feeling' part of me, yes, I think that I'm in touch with my feelings, my emotions. I try to be the best person I can be. I also value my ethics, my rationality, my reasoning processes, my ability to think in sobriety. How would you define spirituality?"

The director, a psychiatrist, said, "Well, yes, spirituality is, I suppose, that interconnectedness we feel with all things. It's . . . really, it's a hard word to define. Perhaps it cannot really be defined, but you'll know it when you experience it." The other Twelve-Step counselors chuckled and nodded knowingly, and we were told that they'd "get back" to us, as a potential SOS meeting bit the dust.

Happily, many chemical-dependency professionals are open to alternatives. The "why" is simple. Alternatives translate into

a greater number of restored human lives. It's that simple—
far simpler than the old (and oftentimes vague) concepts of
the vested interests.

Health agencies (both private and public), clinics, referral
services, organizations, churches, hospitals, and universities, have
contacted SOS, many encouraging us and applauding our
existence. Those interested in the SOS alternative have included
representatives of such diverse organizations as the Delaware
Drinking Driver Program; the State of Washington Department
of Social Health Services; the University of Wisconsin; Storefront
Centers for Counseling, Drug and Alcohol Treatment Systems
(Florida); Security Plan, Member's Assistance Program (New
Jersey); Women's Center of Central Kentucky, Inc.; State
Univeristy of New York at Fredonia; The Alcohol Research Group
(California); Americans for Religious Liberty (Washington, D.C.);
Alfred University (New York); Bradford Alcoholism and Chemical
Dependency Treatment (Alabama); Office of Alcohol and Drug
Abuse Programs (Vermont); The Salvation Army's Clinton House
(California); the American Humanist Association (New York);
Jefferson Community College (Kentucky); ICD Chemical
Dependency Unit (New York); Veteran's Administration Hospital
(Nebraska); the Addiction Research Foundation (Canada); Wake
Forrest University (North Carolina); Veteran's Administration
Medical Center (Virginia); Drug Free Schools Project (Iowa);
Alcoholism and Addictions Program, Duke University (North
Carolina); Department of Rehabilitation (California); Dayton
Psychological Services (Ohio); Department of Adult Probation
(Texas); Project Cork Institute, Dartmouth Medical School (New
Hampshire); Wicomico County Health Department (Maryland);
Office of Mental Health, New York State Psychiatric Institute
(New York); Townhall II Chemical Dependency Treatment

Program (Ohio); Community Care Services (Michigan); Veteran's Administration Medical Center (California); Behavioral Treatment Unit, Northeast Florida State Hospital; L.A. County Office of Alcohol Programs (California); Community Mental Health Center (Washington); Solutions Counseling and Treatment Center (Texas); Community Drug Board (Ohio); Southwest Youth Service Bureau (Washington); Oregon Council on Alcoholism and Drug Addiction; Encyclopedia of Associations (Michigan); University of Denver; New Dawn Recovery Center (Florida); Metropolitan Clinic of Counseling (Virginia); Haight-Ashbury Alcohol Treatment Services (California); Catholic Charities of Buffalo; Family Service of Montgomery County (Pennsylvania); Kent State University (Ohio); Sidney L. Johnson Vocational Center (New York); AIDS Health Service Team, Jersey City Medical Center (New Jersey); Braille Institute (California); Alcohol and Drug Awareness Program, The University of Texas Medical Branch at Galveston; Veteran's Administration Memorial Hospital (Massachusetts); Methodist Pathway Center (Florida); Center for Drug Free Living, Van Etten Hospital (New York); The Single Parent Program, FOCUS Center (California); Stabilization Program for Homeless Alcoholics (Massachusetts); and others too numerous to list here.

Unitarian-Universalist churches have been especially supportive, holding local SOS meetings in New Mexico, Maryland, Georgia, Maine, Louisiana, Wisconsin, Texas, Alabama, Washington, California, and Utah. Queries have come in from many other Unitarian churches all across the country. Humanist, rationalist, and skeptics groups have enthusiastically welcomed the SOS alternative, and some altruistic nonalcoholics have started the ball rolling within their own communities. This has happened, for example, in Illinois, Michigan, Pennsylvania, and New York. A lot of progress has been made in two short years.

LETTERS

Almost immediately after "Sobriety Without Superstition" was published, I began to receive letters: letters of astonishing poignance and power. To read them is to witness the despair into which too many had fallen when they were forced to choose between their moral and intellectual integrity and their addiction; it is also to see how SOS helped many save themselves. Some examples:

I read excerpts from How to Stay Sober *in the August issue of* Freethought Today *and was delighted to find a fellow recovering alcoholic who has had similar experiences and made similar observations about AA. I know of no other recovering members who reject unconditionally the theistic beliefs of their program. I have been a member for more than six years, the last four of which were superstition-free. I have made my viewpoints clear and have directly assailed AA's own brand of mythology in the many meetings I attend. I stand alone.*

Alcoholics Anonymous is its own religion. It has two patriarchs, a bible, and twelve commandments. Its members pray before and after its often ritualistic meetings, and the main body of thought lies in a dogmatic belief that its deity, the Higher Power, will rescue its members from the affliction of alcoholism.

It is a shame that AA chose to dabble in the supernatural, attempting to remedy a very real sickness with a very imaginary cure. Like all beliefs in supernatural beings, the reputations of those beings are Teflon-coated: The misfortunes, calamities, and tragedies that result from belief in them are never attributed to them. While people will gladly attribute their success in staying sober to their Higher Power, when they relapse the omnipotent "HP" is nowhere to be found. Suddenly, relapse is entirely one's own responsibility.

Trust in AA's deity, the Higher Power, can be just as counter-productive and dangerous as a belief in ancient Egypt's Horus, or ancient Rome's Zeus, or modern-day Christianity's Jesus. All are variations on a theme, the "turn it over" theme. All such beliefs seek to answer real-world problems with the vagaries of make-believe. All such theistic beliefs lure their adherents into a false, and therefore dangerous, sense of security. All such beliefs that God will provide teach that one's own drive to find sobriety and the good life is withheld in lieu of divine providence.

Why cannot we be the origin of our sobriety? Why are we not asked to reason, to doubt, to inquire, analyze, challenge, and think? Did the cofounders of AA believe they were capable of providing every answer for every member, even for those who will face problems unimaginable to the limited experiences of a stock broker, a doctor, and the few dozen people whose testimonials are printed in a "big book"?

Sadder still is how AA openly attacks freethinkers, atheists, agnostics, and rationalists. Close-mindedness [leads to] contempt as the "big book" author asserts that "something like half of us thought we were atheists or agnostics"—which implies that our skeptical, philosophical views are things of which we should be cured—that they are in league with our alcoholism.

Those of us with the courage to think for ourselves may formulate new, functional, and superstition-free lifestyles by which to guide and illuminate our lives. We are not waiting for some person, institution, organization, or Holy See to show us a way to happiness. We are quite capable of forging ahead alone or with other members who value rationalism and thought above superstition and faith. Secular Organizations for Sobriety is doing just that.

Indiana

*   *   *

SOS is alive and well in our community. With a core group of ten and a weekly attendance that occasionally reaches seventeen or eighteen, we have an active meeting at the Unitarian-Universalist church.

Our group was formed in December of last year and adopted a format suggested in some of the earlier SOS literature. We have found that a relatively structured meeting, with a clear explanation of our purpose at its start, suits our needs very well. While we hope to spread the word, increase our membership, and eventually spawn other meetings in the area, we are focused on sobriety as our priority above all.

While the subject of AA obviously arises at our meetings, we try to deal with the personal issues that it creates (anger and frustration, for example) and to work on relating these issues to staying sober. "Bad-rapping" AA is a giant waste of time. Sobriety is what we are about. We are happy and fortunate to have two of our members who have begun their sobriety with SOS in our group.

Florida

*   *   *

It was with great pleasure that I read How to Stay Sober. *I have been sober through AA for about three and a half years yet still consider myself an atheist (no small accomplishment, as you well know).*

In the last year or so I have grown increasingly skeptical of the spiritual approach to recovery. The only aspect of AA that has kept me sober was the reinforcement (inherent in AA's fellowship) of the life-and-death importance of sobriety. Still, my feeling of alienation in AA had grown to such a proportion that I planned to leave the fellowship and attempt some controlled drinking. After reading your book, that (potentially disastrous) compulsion left me, and I made plans to either find or start an SOS group.

Thank you for having the courage to pioneer an alternative to AA for those of us who see nothing but dependency, superstition, mindlessness, and sedation in a "religious" approach to recovery.

New Jersey

*   *   *

I was more than pleased to learn of SOS. It was such a relief to finally have a conversation with another recovering alcoholic where I felt open and comfortable about my "heresy."

Being put off by the religious/cultish character of AA, I have stayed in the background during my four years of sobriety. I do not work "steps," rarely "share" at meetings, and have not made AA friends. Consequently, I miss out on that wonderful sense of belonging and community that the more orthodox members of AA seem to enjoy.

It is a painful irony: AA should have been the perfect place for me to deal with the neuroses and anxieties that surfaced when

I first got clean and sober. Instead, my recovery has been in limbo. I don't drink or use—but I have been withdrawn, anxious, and lonely the past four years. Fortunately, I have just begun professional counseling to help with that. The next step is to find a support group that I can relate to.

Which brings me to one of the reasons for writing: I would be delighted to consider myself a member of SOS and offer whatever support I can to get a group going in the paradise of Hawaii, if there is not a group here already.

Finally, please accept my thanks and appreciation for your work with SOS. It must have taken a lot of guts to buck the system— but I guess you are aware you are addressing an important and unmet need. I am certain there are many others who, like me, have fallen through the cracks of the AA establishment and really want an alternative.

Hawaii

*   *   *

Although I have been sober in the fellowship of Alcoholics Anonymous for three years, I have felt all along the need for a secular recovery group. I have never been confortable with the be-absolved-of-your-sins approach of the Twelve-Step groups, and you are well aware that much of the AA orthodoxy flies in the face of our growing knowledge of alcoholism as a physiological disease.

New York

*   *   *

I too am an alcoholic (sober ten months) and I am an agnostic. Like you, I appreciated the support of AA, but I have become more and more alienated from it. One meeting, when the topic was "higher power," I described myself as a nonbeliever; my sense of fellowship, I said, was my higher power. At the end of the meeting the chair asked me to lead the Lord's Prayer!

Vermont

*   *   *

I noticed your address in the February issue of Glamour, I have been attending C.A. [Cocaine Anonymous] meetings since March 1988, and while I find them helpful from a group-therapy standpoint, I am uneasy about the Lord's Prayer, Third-Step Prayer, and the constant references to God and "What HE has done for me. . . ." I have attempted "working the steps," but find the third step to be my roadblock, since I don't know what sort of "higher power" I should be turning my will and life over to the care of. Others have told me that prayer would come easier if I had a clear idea of what my higher power is—even if it's a chair!

I guess I'm not sure the answers are to be found outside myself; they should be found in myself, as a part of myself.

Ohio

*   *   *

In Oregon, those arrested for "driving while under the influence" are often ordered to attend sessions of commercial groups for treating alcoholics or to Alcoholics Anonymous. We receive many complaints that people *so ordered are subjected to religious teachings or told that the only way to recovery is to accept religion.*

A.C.L.U. of Oregon

*   *   *

I went through an alcohol-rehabilitation program with my spouse (he was the alcoholic, I the codependent). Three months and some $3,600 later, all they could tell us was to keep going to AA and Al-Anon. When I asked about the blatantly King-James-version religious nature of the Twelve Steps, I was told to read the chapter in the Big Book about agnostics. I was also told to "fake it till you make it."

My alcoholic is still struggling with AA, and I am still struggling with Al-Anon. I cannot say that no good has come from our associations with these religious groups, but I can and do say that what progress we have made need not have come at such a terrific effort. I have had to struggle to be true to my own beliefs. I am a devout and devoted agnostic Unitarian-Universalist. I and four others with similar views formed our own Al-Anon group so that we would not have to do any praying. We are of course not registered with Al-Anon headquarters in New York for fear of being rejected.

Here in the Bible Belt, SOS is the only light burning in the oppressively dark night of Christian Fundamentalism for those with alcohol and codependency problems who also have liberal religious views. I hope that SOS continues to grow and develop and that there is eventually an SOS group here. To keep the hope alive, we need that newsletter.

Arkansas

*   *   *

When I noticed your folder in a library here today, it was with such an intense delight. That must sound a little strange to you. Let me explain.

In my decades as a social worker I've counseled many alcoholics. It has always pleased me when one of them decided to enter AA. But I've been equally pleased later on if he or she outgrew it. Replacing one addiction with another is not the way to go.

Florida

*   *   *

I read about SOS in the Utne Reader, and my heart lifted. . . . I have yet to find an AA group that doesn't open and close with either the Lord's Prayer or the Serenity Prayer (equally objectionable to me). Although there are certain somewhat sophisticated intellectual groups in New York, one is always apt to be exposed to the "how I found God and got sober" syndrome. Most groups are tolerant of my counter-view. They tell me, "Take what you can use and leave the rest" or "Keep coming back." But I am nonetheless made uncomfortable, and I worry that I still have a "denial" factor in myself. I no longer drink, but I'd be glad to be in a discussion group of nonreligious alcoholics.

New York

*   *   *

I have been attending Overeaters Anonymous meetings for about six weeks. I agree that more than just a diet is needed to cure compulsive overeating, but as a person with a science background, the religious nature of OA is not for me. Is there an OA equivalent to the Secular Organizations for Sobriety?

Virginia

*   *   *

As an addictions educator and researcher, as well as a secular humanist, I am exasperated by the chemical-dependency industry's addiction to promoting "spiritual" paths to recovery as the only effective paths. Because most addicted individuals never enter any formal recovery program, and because most of those who do have major problems with relapse, there is a clear need for new approaches to recovery. Your SOS idea has great potential for meeting the needs of those who don't or won't recover in "spiritually" oriented programs.

I would like to present your program in my course, "Addictive Behaviors and Treatment Issues."

Kent State University, Ohio

*   *   *

I have worked with alcoholics for over twenty years as a clinical psychologist and currently lecture to groups of human-service professionals who are trying to learn more about the issues associated with alcoholics. Based upon my work with patients and my reading of the alcoholism research literature, I concluded a number of years ago that alternatives to AA were needed. The approach you describe seems a reasonable and needed one.

Georgia State University, Georgia

*   *   *

I am a director of a federally sponsored program that works with low-income, "multi-problemed," high-risk child abusive families. Our preferred approach in working with families is to "empower" our clients to deal with reality. Our "empowerment" service model is consistent with almost all credible helping approaches practiced today, except the AA approach, which I feel is in opposition to ours.

Wisconsin

*   *   *

I have been recovering since May of 1982. I looked for a secular alternative to AA at that time, but there simply wasn't any. I happen to be nontheist, and for obvious reasons found AA in many ways to be more alienating than my alcoholism. Recovery is tough enough without having to spend a lot of mental energy resisting scads of religiously oriented dogmatic material about surrendering control of your life to some "Higher Power" that you don't believe exists. I would be interested in starting an SOS meeting in this area.

California

*   *   *

SOS is just about the only hope for anyone seeking a rational basis for abstinence and sobriety. AA attracts those happy with the faith-healing formula. Right now the AA mind-set controls most alcoholism treatment. *The detox and rehab centers, even if they really know better, have to go along to get the business.*

New York

*   *   *

As a three-year veteran of Al-Anon and an attendee of AA meetings, the religion inherent in that program puts me off. They stress that it is a spiritual program, not a religious one, and then they say the Lord's Prayer at the end of every meeting. I have met no one in these meetings who sees a contradiction there. Since the rise of the "Born Again" movement, there is also a lot of talk about Jesus in some of the meetings, and in many cases no one objects.

Now, I will continue to spread the word. There is a definite need for SOS.

Arizona

*   *   *

SOS is of interest to me both professionally and personally. Professionally, I have always resented the apparent monopoly of alcoholic-recovery programs long claimed by Alcoholics Anonymous—especially the need for a total reliance on the "Higher Power." I wondered if it wasn't a case of trading a chemical dependency for an emotional-religious one.

California

*   *   *

I am a nontheist, a humanist, a recovered alcoholic, and a potential SOS convener. I first entered an AA treatment center in the early 1970s. It was a miserable experience and a total failure. I lasted less than two weeks simply because I would not allow them to denigrate or humiliate me. I know many who try to overlook the religiosity of AA, and know of more than a few who could not handle it and walked away from the AA meeting and into the closest bar!

Minnesota

*   *   *

I have been struggling with the philosophy of Alcoholics Anonymous since 1976, and recently I have begun to struggle with what is becoming a more and more frankly religious spirit spreading through that fellowship. There is now a "concordance" to the AA Big Book—making it at last the "sacred scripture" that many members have always wanted it to be.

I'm tired of being told alcoholism is a "disease" of the body, mind, and spirit—but that the mind has no apparent right to recover. I'm tired of being told that to object to naming alcoholism a disease is being "too intellectual," and being accused of "debating" when I observe that the disease concept is itself an intellectual model.

I know religious truths when I see them, and the Twelve Steps are a program of Christian "moral rearmament" in disguise. I do not desire to become a moral and upright citizen of a quietly subservient Christian commonwealth. I desire only to break the cycle of addiction that has caused such misery in my life and to do it in the company of others who have had the same difficulty.

Massachusetts

*   *   *

It is the most wonderful feeling in the world—like having a good long drink of cold clear water after you've exercised long and hard— to have another person confirm for you that you're not alone in your misgivings about something so sacred as the AA program. SOS is an oasis in the desert!

Georgia

*   *   *

I am a disabled veteran recovering from a very serious alcohol problem. Like many other atheists with similar problems, I fell into the trap of AA largely from desperation and the pressure of family and doctors. The impact of the AA cult on my life was almost devastating. Its Twelve Steps are nothing more than the old Roman Catholic penance system, which instills pathological delusions of sin and guilt in its victims.

Florida

*   *   *

It seems that SOS is needed more and more around here, at least by me. I learned one thing in the past few weeks: It isn't fun to try to spread the message of SOS at a meeting that is held in a church basement and is dominated by devout, Roman Catholic, sober "saints." I made two brief announcements that I was not promoting SOS but simply providing information. Imagine my frustration, rage, and disappointment when my own sponsor (now former sponsor) later admitted that he had trashed the SOS literature. His reasons? SOS isn't AA, and the room is an AA room. This is nonsense, as there is all kinds of non-AA literature there, and the room is owned by the church, not by AA.

In short, I have had it with being harassed in meetings because I dare not to follow the AA party line on religion. I have my own deeply held religious beliefs, founded partly on my Native American heritage and partly on Zen. This is beside the point, however, since I believe that one's recovery should be kept apart from one's religion, whatever it may be.

Having read the Big Book "religiously" over the past months, I now realize how important SOS is. I have taken a few tentative steps towards starting two SOS groups in my area. I will keep you posted on progress.

Meanwhile, I am staying clean and sober in spite of AA, not because of it. Whenever I have needed help because my own personal resources were not enough, there was neither "burning bush" nor deus ex machina in evidence. I got all my help from people.

Pennsylvania

*   *   *

Two facts that AA members like to ignore: Most people are religious, and AA is usually the last resort for most people. Taken together, the result is that most people, long before even considering AA, tried everything else, including going to church and turning their alcoholic problem over to God as they understood Him. And, it didn't work. If it had, none of these people would ever have ended up in AA.

Religious insanity is a poor substitute for alcoholic insanity. It involves the same kind of denial of reality, self-deception, and substitution of delusion for reality that alcoholic insanity involves. Alcoholics need *to get away from this.*

I don't ask spooks for anything in the morning, converse with them at lunch, or thank them at night. Nowhere but in the human imagination do spooks or the supernatural exist. They don't exist in mine.

Texas

*   *   *

I've gone through a pretty tumultuous last couple of weeks, with much soul-searching and discussions with . . . a trusted psychologist. The upshot: I don't want to continue with the A.C.A. (Adult Children of Alcoholics) program unless I can find (or help start) a secular support group here.

I can see where the regular Twelve Steps based on AA can be useful and maybe even necessary to someone who is battling a truly life-and-death chemical addiction (although SOS has shown me that there are alternatives), but I have come to doubt the appropriateness of applying that addiction-oriented approach to anything and everything that ails the human race. My psychologist believes that the regular Twelve Steps are substituting one form of addiction for another . . . .

About this whole idea of "God as we understand Him"—While I feel that in theory this might be able to work as a place-holder for general "higher powers," in practice the whole slant of the conventional Twelve Steps embodies the Judeo/Christian God. Of course, the devout Christians in my step study group can't see this at all. ("The fish never notices the water it swims in," or something like that.)

My psychologist confirmed for me that I had progressed far enough to have a certain sophistication in spotting the games being played, and that this was contributing to my discomfort. One of the games is the basic Christian control scam, if I may call it that, which harks

*back to that "no way to the Father except through me" attitude.
No way to recovery except turning over your will and life to the Higher
Power—and if you believe that that's unhealthy, ipso facto you are
"in denial." There is a definite cultishness about that type of closed-
system thinking, which sets off my danger alarms (which are healthy
protective instincts, I say).*

*I had been going along, trying to "take what I need and leave
the rest," and translating unacceptable ideas (and the Lord's Prayer)
into something I could live with—but the effort has been immense.
My psychologist astutely observed that that was just recreating the typical
alcoholic family pattern of doublespeak and doublethink—having to
deal with one thing on the surface and another underneath. I had
been wrestling with my gut-level instincts, which said it would be healthier
for me not to put myself in situations like that when I have a choice
in the matter. Of course, my step study group looked very smug and
said it was proof of denial, but my psychologist (who is a helluva
lot better equipped to judge, I think) validated my assessment. . . .
The conventional Twelve Steps seem to imply that the ego is a naughty,
rebellious child that can't do anything right unless the Big Daddy in
the Sky is in control!*

*Fundamentally, there's a familiar existential problem here. Facing
a world where we make our own destiny, where there's no omnipotent
power looking out for us personally and making a wonderful plan for
our very own little lives, is admittedly a lot scarier and less comforting
than the hears-every-falling-sparrow idea of God. But I don't choose
to live in a fool's paradise. If I need reassurance and comfort, I can
turn to friends, my dogs, or my teddy bear, none of whom require
me to adopt a stance of powerlessness or turn my brain into mush.*

California

*   *   *

First, I am very pleased to inform you that I have started a new SOS group. Our first meeting was held on Monday, May 15, 1989. Nine people attended, and enthusiasm abounded. Our second meeting was held on Wednesday, May 24. Eight people attended. Again, the group was both enthusiastic and deeply appreciative of the fact that a nonreligious recovery support group was available.

We now have a core group of about twelve. However, some members can attend on Mondays but not Wednesdays. The reverse is also true. Beginning in June, we will be holding meetings on both Monday and Wednesday evenings. Our format is very loosely structured. At each meeting, a designated member opens with a brief reading of his or her choice. That reading then serves as a focal point for discussion. However, any member who has a pressing issue to discuss (especially something that he or she deems to be sobriety-threatening) is encouraged to discuss that issue. On Wednesday night, I read a few paragraphs from Viktor Frankl's Man's Search For Meaning.

I would like to recount the travails that I have encountered in starting an SOS group in my community. Feel free to reprint any part of my saga. If you choose not to use my letter, at least you will have given me an opportunity to vent my feelings.

In your newsletter of August/September 1988, you stated, "All that is really required to start a group is a place to meet." Based on my experience, I believe that the above statement is only partially true. For our group, securing a rent-free meeting place at a local public junior high school required almost no effort at all. What was really required to start an SOS group was both a stomach and a psyche that were strong enough to endure the public vilification and scorn of the local AA establishment.

I want to preface my chronicle by telling you that I have been

*a law professor at a nearby university for more than a decade. Prior
to that, I was a trial lawyer for the U.S. Department of Justice.
I mention these facts not because I wish to establish my academic
and professional credentials. Rather, I want you to understand that,
both by training and by inclination, I am very assertive and am rarely
daunted or intimidated by verbal attacks.*

*Approximately five years ago, I first realized that I had a serious
problem with alcohol. I immediately joined AA, and have been floating
in and out—mostly out—of that "fellowship" ever since. In essence,
I had three problems with AA's "program."*

*First, as a life-long agnostic and secular humanist, I was simply
incapable of turning "my life and my will over to the care of God
as I understand Him." I've never understood Him, and I stopped trying
when I was approximately fifteen years old.*

*Second, I saw AA's Twelve Steps as an abdication of personal
responsibility. I believe that each person is responsible for his or her
own successes and failures—including successes and failures in maintaining
sobriety. If I succeed, I will not give the credit to any power "greater
than myself"; and if I fail, I refuse to "pin the rap" on some mythical
deity. My dilemma, however, was that I desperately desired a support
group. I have several wonderful friends, but none is a recovering alcoholic
or addict.*

*Third, although I am religiously (or, rather, irreligiously) an agnostic,
I was raised as a Jew, and I still have strong cultural and ethnic
ties to Judaism. During my last several months in AA (before anyone
knew that I had decided to convene an SOS group) antisemitism became
fashionable in some local AA groups. The "tables" were suddenly replete
with persons who enjoyed engaging in antisemitic slurs and telling
antisemitic jokes. Each time this occurred, I would wait until it was
my turn to speak. Instead of the usual introduction ("My name is
Jane, and I'm an alcoholic"), I would begin with: "My name is Jane,*

and I'm a Jew." I would then protest the blatant antisemitism within the "fellowship." Only one person, a woman from a Christian background, was empathetic and expressed her outrage. I am delighted to report that she became the second charter member of my SOS group.

On all other occasions when I raised the anitsemitism issue, the group rejoinder was always the same. I was told that I was "sitting on the pity pot" and/or that I didn't have a sense of humor. I told the group that these two responses were patently absurd. First, I was not engaging in self-pity. I am extremely proud of my Jewish heritage. Second, since I don't see anything funny about religious or ethnic bigotry, I probably did not, by group standards, have a sense of humor.

I found the newly emerging antisemitism within some local AA groups to be not only upsetting but also puzzling. After all, one of AA's well-known cliches is "live and let live." In addition, we all lived in a university community, an (alleged) bastion for "liberal" thought and deed. Yet, after several such episodes, and because of my life-long commitment to nontheism, I knew that it was time for SOS to arrive in this community.

When I first became determined to convene an SOS group, I decided that I would simply submit releases to the local press. I rented a post office box and, using your suggested wording, ran a weekly announcement in the local newspaper. The response was nil; my disappointment was great. I then ran an ad in the May issue of a monthly magazine that is read by virtually everyone who lives in this city and the surrounding areas. I simultaneously reserved a room at a local junior high school for our first meeting. On Monday, May 15 (a date that I chose at random).

The response to my ad in the magazine was also somewhat disappointing. I received six replies. However, some of the respondents, upon learning that "we" would not be affiliated with AA or any other twelve-step program, stated that they were not interested. Only one *woman said that she would attend. She did.*

By May 12, three days before the first scheduled SOS meeting, I realized that time was running out. I read and reread James Christopher's account of his sense of virtual aloneness in trying to convene the very first SOS meetings. He wrote: "For many weeks, despite attempts to spread the message with flyers and word of mouth, that dear lady (an agnostic with a Jewish background) and I held most of the meetings for each other only."

I did not want to repeat Mr. Christopher's experience. While I admire him greatly, I possess neither his tenacity, his optimism, nor his tolerance for disappointment.

Thus, on the evening of Friday, May 12, I showed up at an AA meeting that I knew would be very heavily attended. When the group leader asked if there were any "AA-related announcements," I spoke. My statement was, in essence, as follows: "A new sobriety group is being formed. It is open to all recovering alcoholics and addicts, but is especially designed for atheists, agnostics, and persons who are just plainly skeptical." (I then gave the date, time, and place of the first meeting.) I continued: "If you feel that you might be comfortable at such a meeting, or if you are just simply curious, please join us."

My announcement was greeted with a gale of laughter. I spoke again. I said, as poignantly as possible (and trying not to reveal my anger): "Please don't laugh. I consider alcoholism and drug addiction to be life-and-death matters. Many alcoholics and addicts come to AA. They perceive, rightly or wrongly, that it is a religious organization; they leave. We don't know what happens to most of them. Probably some of them recover, and some of them die. My brother was a drug addict. During a brief period when he was clean and sober, he attended AA. He felt deeply alienated by what he perceived to be the religiosity of the organization. Perhaps that was just his excuse to continue using drugs. Perhaps not. I will never know; nor will anyone else. He left

AA, and he died a few months later at the age of thirty-four."

No one dared laugh. The meeting continued, and I remained silent throughout.

Two days later (a Sunday, and the day before the first scheduled SOS meeting) I once again appeared at a heavily attended AA meeting. This time, I not only made my announcement but also placed flyers on all the tables approximately fifteen minutes before the meeting began. Immediately after placing flyers on the tables, I watched as one man tore several of them into shreds. Instead of venting my anger (which was very intense and extremely visceral), I immediately put on my actress persona. I went up to him, gave him an AA-type hug, and said, "I'm sorry you're not feeling well today. I'm concerned about you." He looked perplexed. I continued, "You must be feeling very insecure, or you wouldn't have felt the need to tear up a harmless piece of paper." He replied, "It's not a harmless piece of paper," and walked away.

The following evening, my SOS group held its first meeting. During the next six days, I appeared at several AA meetings, continued to place our SOS flyers on the tables, made very brief announcements, and always remained to attend the AA meeting itself. At two such meetings, the group with which I sat chose "resentment" as its topic. Most (but certainly not all) of the persons would then express their resentment towards me and SOS. My response on both occasions was: "I don't understand your resentment. For every alcoholic and addict, recovery is a life-and-death issue. If one achieves sobriety through AA or NA, I applaud him or her. If one achieves sobriety through an alternative recovery group such as SOS, I applaud him or her. If one achieves sobriety through years of expensive and painstaking psychotherapy, I applaud him or her. And finally, if one achieves sobriety simply by standing up one morning and saying, 'I will not put any more toxins into my system,' and adheres to that decision, I applaud him or her. *All roads to recovery are equally valid and equally worthy of praise.*"

On both occasions there was an ensuing discussion about whether people in a "*valueless*" recovery program were "*truly sober*" or simply "*dry drunks.*" (*The latter is a term which I have* never *understood*). I explained that neither I nor any of the people I had met in SOS were without values. Our values, however, were based on a system that emphasized man's humanity to man; our ethics did not flow from any deity. This generally fell on deaf ears, but in one instance it piqued the interest of two AA members, who subsequently showed up at the second SOS meeting.

The denouement occurred on Sunday, May 21. Upon arriving at an early morning meeting, I noticed that several of our flyers had been defaced by graffiti. On one of them someone had written, "*Surrender to God, you asshole.*" (*I must admit that eloquence of style has always impressed me.*) On another flyer someone had scribbled a more pernicious message: "*If you don't like AA, why don't you just go out and get drunk?*"

When that meeting began, and the moderator asked for announcements, I once again announced our forthcoming meeting and registered a rather mild protest over the defacement of our circulars. The moderator said, "*Sit down and shut up. Your announcement has nothing to do with AA.*" I knew at that moment that our "*time was up,*" but I was happy that for nine days we had been able to use AA meetings as a forum (albeit a generally hostile one) for our flyers and oral announcements.

At the end of that meeting, I was approached by a man who is the "*Lord-High-Everything-Else*" of the local AA. He said that, on behalf of AA, he must ask me to desist from making announcements or passing out flyers regarding SOS. I politely acquiesced. He said, "*I expected you to argue with me.*" I replied, "*No, you are perfectly within your rights. As long as AA remains a purely private organization, and is not allied with any part of the government such as the courts, you are free to trammel the Constitutional rights of SOS and all its members. These include our freedom of speech, our freedom of association, our freedom of religion, and our freedom from religion."*

The man looked rather chagrined, and replied, "I don't see this as a legal issue; I see it as a matter of ethics." I responded, "I agree with you. But your code of ethics is very different from ours."

"In what way?" he asked.

"Well, for openers, you seem determined to infringe on our personal liberties, whereas we have no interest in encroaching upon yours." (End of conversation.)

I have had no further contact with AA or any of its members, with the exception, of course, of those who have attended SOS meetings. I am not a secular Joan of Arc, and I have no taste for martyrdom. Moreover, not all members of the AA community have reacted to SOS with hostility. Some have been very supportive. Two members of the AA establishment have actually told nontheist alcoholics and addicts about the existence of SOS, and have given such persons my phone number.

Meanwhile, I am relatively certain that our local SOS group will grow and thrive. We are receiving at least one inquiry per day, either by phone or by mail. In addition, I have been in touch with an excellent lawyer whose entire practice consists of handling drunk-driving cases. He was very interested to learn of the existence of SOS, since many of his clients object to AA on religious grounds. We also plan to contact the local broadcast media.

I want to close by expressing my deepest appreciation to all of you, particularly James Christopher. I am going through a period of great stress and turmoil in my personal life. But, simply knowing of the existence of SOS, and becoming the convener of (a local) group, has helped me to maintain my equanimity. Indeed, it has become my raison d'etre.

Michigan

THE SOS MEETING

The following is a condensed fictionalized recreation of an SOS meeting. These grassroots group meetings are generally one and a half hours in length, with a ten-to-fifteen-minute coffee break halfway through the meeting. You're welcome to join us now, and we hope to see you again next week.

*   *   *

Jack: Welcome to SOS. My name is Jack, a sober alcoholic, and I've been asked to lead tonight's meeting.

Secular Organizations for Sobriety/Save Our Selves is dedicated to providing a path to sobriety that is an alternative to those paths depending upon supernatural or religious beliefs. We respect diversity, welcome healthy skepticism, encourage rational thinking as well as the expression of our feelings, and we each take responsibility for our individual sobriety daily.

This is a sobriety meeting. Our focus is on the priority of abstaining from alcohol and other mind-altering drugs.

We respect the anonymity of each person in this room. This is a self-help, nonprofessional group. At this meeting we share our experiences, understandings, thoughts, and feelings.

Are there any announcements? [At this point, Jack announces that there's literature available over on the table, and he notes the schedule of SOS and Families-and-Friends group meetings.]

We celebrate various lengths of sobriety in these meetings. Is there anyone here with under thirty days of continuous sobriety? Sixty days . . . ninety days . . . six months . . . nine months? Is anyone celebrating a yearly anniversary tonight? If you have an anniversary date coming up, please let me know after the meeting and we'll prepare a celebration for that date.

Tonight I have asked Judy to read the suggested Guidelines for Sobriety.

Judy: To break the cycle of denial and achieve sobriety, we first acknowledge that we are alcoholics/addicts.

* We reaffirm this truth daily and accept without reservation— one day at a time—the fact that as clean and sober individuals, we cannot and do not drink or use, *no matter what.*

* Since drinking/using is not an option for us, we take whatever steps are necessary to continue our Sobriety Priority lifelong.

* We can achieve "the good life." However, life is also filled with uncertainties; therefore, we do not drink/use regardless of feelings, circumstances, or conflicts.

* We share in confidence with each other our thoughts and feelings as sober, clean individuals.

* Sobriety is our Priority, and we are each responsible for our lives and our sobriety.

Jack: Starting with the person on my left, let's introduce ourselves. Again, I'm Jack, sober alcoholic.

Fred: Hi. I'm Fred, sober alcoholic.

Gil: I'm Gil, former drunk.

Judy: Hi, Gil! My name is Judy, I'm a sober alcoholic.

Karla: Karla, recovering alcoholic/addict.

Patti: Patti, addict/alcoholic, sober.

Mark: I'm Mark, and I've got a problem with alcohol. . . .

Phyllis: Phyllis . . .

Al: Al . . . our daughter's on drugs and alcohol. . . .

Jack: And I'm still Jack, a sober alcoholic. This meeting is now open. We ask that you try to keep your sharing to a reasonable length of time so that everyone can participate. We're smaller in number tonight, though, so it looks like there'll be ample time for everyone. Oh, yes, crosstalk is okay in this meeting. We take a coffee break about halfway. There's no smoking allowed in this building, but you can smoke outside the door there at break-time.

Well, I don't really have any particular topic, except . . . we could talk about . . . how about "relationships in sobriety"? And anything else you want to talk about tonight.

I'll start by saying that my relationships with other people, now that I've been continuously sober for seven years, are far better than when I was drinking. I was a "functioning drunk." I had a job and went to work every day, except on those days that I supposedly had "the flu" or "car trouble" or "a death in the family" or whatever excuses I concocted to tell my boss because of my monster hangovers. Anyway, my troubles in my sober life are really so much easier to deal with nowadays. I feel anxious around new people sometimes. Other times I feel pretty relaxed. I feel my feelings and I feel like I'm living authentically today, in sobriety. Sure, people get to me at times. They can piss me off. When people "do me wrong"—or at least, from my perspective, I see it that way—I don't think of a drink. I sometimes wish I could run away from the circumstances in my life, but this is only momentary. I tend to my sobriety daily by prioritizing it as a separate issue, and I get a lot of freedom . . . liberation from that.

Anyway, human relationships can be a sonofabitch. My girlfriend has really been giving me a hard time lately.

Gil: Poor baby!

Jack: Yeah, well, my girlfriend Susan has some very definite ideas that don't always correspond with mine, and *vice versa.* We've got a lot in common but she can be a real pain in the ass at times. But, so can I. Just saying this out loud makes me feel better. Anyway, I want to build something with her. I want to acknowledge her needs, I really respect her. Sometimes I try to control her, and I think she does the same thing with me at times, too. We've had some clashes lately, more so than usual. Her job is really getting her down, and I've been irritable and edgy from the pressures at my work, too. Got a new boss now and he is driving the staff batty. He's a perfectionist. But I'm that way too, sometimes. Anyway, I feel better talking about this tonight. Thanks for letting me share. Gil?

Gil: Relationships in sobriety, huh? Well, funny you should suggest that particular topic tonight. Five years ago the only relationship left to me was "the bottle." I watched the television test pattern, or, I should say, I had an intense relationship with the television test pattern and my filthy apartment and the liquor store's delivery service. Everyone else had bowed out of my life. My ex-wife took our two kids and left the state. My employer gave me a pink slip and I lived off credit cards until they were taken away from me. My blood pressure was sky high and I felt like hell. Looked like hell, too. So I ran out of everything, including relationships. I had a few sleazy contacts when I'd venture out to the neighborhood bar, but at the end of my drinking I preferred my apartment.

When I first got sober, I went to some AA meetings, pretty shaky. The "God Stuff" turned me off but I found some caring people there. I still attend AA today; glad it's there. But I really "get off" on this meeting with all my fellow heretics. Just kidding. Relationships? I actually have them today. My new lady and I will probably get married in about six months. We work together in a pretty successful little business today. She's really been a "godsend," pardon the expression, and she and I get along

really well . . . most of the time. This is all "gravy" for me
since I really had no life to speak of, especially toward the
last three or four years of my drinking. I even get along with
my mom today. She knows that I won't put up with too much
crap from her now that I'm sober. Yeah, relationships are for
the most part good today. Glad to be here tonight. Glad to
be sober, and thanks.

Jack: Thanks, Gil. Judy?

Judy: Judy, sober alcoholic. Well, let's see . . . I didn't think
you'd call on me, but . . . about relationships . . . I liked what
you said, Gil, in that I had no relationships left as my alcoholism
progressed. In my twenty-two months of sobriety I've met some
really fine people, and they like me. I'm no longer a nonentity.
See . . . that's what I felt like, about myself, when I drank.
I just looked at the tabletop in the bars I went to. I didn't
speak to anyone. Eventually, just before "last call," some bastard
would take me home to his place and I'd wake up the next
morning with less self-respect than I had the night before, if
that's possible. This went on and on. That was my life. Stuck
in a dead-end job. My friends would cover for me. I could
get away with stuff, missing days at work, because I did good
work when I worked, but I never really credited myself for
that. Or anything else, for that matter.

    People said I was pretty, but I didn't believe them. Besides,
I felt like all I had was that, at least some looks, not much
else. I started boozing when I was sixteen, at my Dad's bar.
He died soon after, of alcoholism. Guess it never occurred to
me that I carried it in my genes. Well, in the beginning of

my drinking I felt pretty hot. The guys liked me. In reality, I was just an easy lay.

As my alcoholism progressed, I really had less and less self-esteem. I had a secret dream of being a newspaper reporter but, like I said, I never tried. I just kept these nowhere jobs, office work, and paid my rent and drank away my dreams. And I got pregnant in the process. Had an abortion. With all the booze in my system at the time of my pregnancy, that was a good decision. I met a guy later who drank like I did. We'd polish off a gallon of wine on a slow evening, and our "relationship" lasted for over a year until he came at me one night with a table lamp. I had some minor injuries, but fortunately he slipped on the hall rug and I got away. That was the end of that. The next day I started going to AA meetings, and, after I heard about SOS, I began coming here.

Well, lots has happened for me in sobriety. I'm enrolled in a journalism class in college, I've been promoted at my job—more money—but I'm also closer to my dream of eventually working as a newspaper reporter. I've had lots of encouragement from my teachers and have had two of my articles published in the local papers. I've got a real relationship today with a guy I met at college. I feel good about me today. Thanks for calling on me and I'm glad I'm here.

Jack: Thank you, Judy . . . .

Phillis: I really need to talk . . . .

Jack: Sure, go ahead.

Phyllis: I'm Phyllis, and I'm here tonight with my husband.

Al: I'm Al, we're . . . this is our first SOS meeting. Phyllis saw the announcement in the local paper about this secular meeting and we're . . . oh, honey, it's okay, baby . . . .

Karla: Here, Phyllis, take this one. I've got a whole packet.

Phyllis: Thanks. I appreciate you folks being here and . . . thanks for the tissue.

Karla: Anytime. There's more if you need 'em.

Phyllis: I didn't mean to break down but . . . I just . . . I don't know how much longer . . . how much more of this . . . Our daughter is an alcoholic and she's . . . a heroin . . . she's . . . . God, she's been taking drugs for God knows how long. I knew she had a problem with alcohol, at least it seemed like it. Her friends . . . she left with these friends about a month ago. Left a note and we've only had two phone calls since then. She's living with a dealer, from what we've been able to find out. She's over eighteen. Legally she's an adult . . . .

Patti: Phyllis, I'm Patti, and I'm a sober addict and an alcoholic. I came through a rehab program over three years ago, and before that I was selling myself as a prostitute in order to get a fix. At break time I can give you the names of some people who can help you get help for your daughter . . . information to help when your daughter's ready. I say that because my mom had to give up on me, although it almost killed her. She'd give me money. I made promises. I used her money to buy drugs. Heroin, coke, you name it, I took it. Fortunately I never progressed to needles. I'm clean and sober today partially because my mom stopped "enabling" me. When I worked the streets I hit bottom pretty fast and my mom helped get me into this rehab place. . . . You've both got a right to your own lives. We're here for you and we know it hurts. But life goes on. And there is hope.

Phyllis: Thanks, Patti.

Patti: Like you, Judy, my self-esteem was nil. I found that I couldn't stop drinking or using. Now, with a little over three years of sobriety, I've got a lot going for me. I'm not a helpless, powerless blob today. I work in a lawyer's office where there's a lot of pressure. It's really exciting for me. I'm really needed. I have a great relationship with my coworkers. My mom and I are friends today. I've been in touch with my older sister. She's married and lives in Canada. We're all getting together this summer, my mom included.

I'm really grateful to my mom, Phyllis. She went through a living hell. I was in hell, too, but so was she. Our relationship today is the best.

I don't know about marriage yet, but Bob, my boyfriend, is really growing on me. He wants to get married and I do, too, eventually, so we'll see. He's never used drugs. Once in a while he'll have a glass of wine. You know, a nonalcoholic. He knows all about me. We don't keep stuff from each other. My mom really likes Bob. She's like his advance man, and that's okay.

I'm not here to say my life is all rosebuds; it's not. But having a real life is exciting for me. I've got some power today. I'm a real person with real challenges. As long as I keep my sobriety my number one, separate issue in my daily life, I've got it made!

Phyllis and Al, I'm gonna give you my mom's phone number later at the break. Call her. She knows what you're going through 'cause she's been there. She's a great lady. I used to call her a bitch and lots of other names when I was drinking, especially when she wouldn't meet my demands for money for drugs. "Better living through chemistry" is not my nightmare now. Okay, I'll shut up. Thanks.

Jack: Thanks, Patti. Phyllis, I want to encourage you to take one of our meeting lists from the literature table. You're welcome at all our meetings, and our Families and Friends of Alcoholics and Addicts Group meets every Wednesday. I want to encourage you both to check out that meeting. There are folks there who've been through similar experiences and I think you'll find lots of support there.

Al: Thanks, Jack. Thank you all for listening.

Jack: I forgot to mention—check our phone-tree list during the break and add your names to it. First names and phone numbers are fine, and feel free to copy off any names to call from our phone tree. This is especially important for newly sober people in their first thirty days.

Mark: I'd like to say something.

Jack: Go right ahead, Mark.

Mark: I haven't had a drink for six days now.

Jack: Congratulations, Mark, and welcome. Let's give Mark a hand for being here tonight.

Mark: Thanks. I . . . feel that . . . I want to do something about my drinking. It's been getting really out of hand. I got your meeting address from someone at an AA meeting when I told him about my difficulty regarding their insistence on a belief in a Higher Power as a prerequisite to sobriety. He was a good guy. Glad I ran into him because the others seemed to be pretty much into the religious thing, and that's okay; it's just not for me. Like I said, I know I've got a problem with drinking, but I can't buy the other stuff. The SOS concepts make sense to me, and I really feel comfortable here. I've already been to one of your other meetings a couple days ago and I really felt good there, too. I'm new at this. Okay if I go on?

Jack: Sure, that's why we're here.

Mark: I'm gonna lose my job if this keeps up. I work for a large corporation and my boss has warned me pretty good . . . I set my kitchen on fire last week. . . . Yeah, I have to pay attention to this stuff. I can't keep rationalizing it away anymore. I've lost lots of time at work. I've alienated my best friend . . . he's my lover, actually. I'm gay. I was afraid to share this here. Anyway, like I said, I know I've got to do this for myself, not for my lover or my boss or my parents, but for me. I guess I could use one of those tissues, Karla.

Karla: Glad to oblige. Here, take two.

Mark: Yeah, thanks. What I'm . . . Goddamn it, what I want to say is . . . I . . . am . . . an alcoholic.

Jack: It's okay, Mark. Take all the time you need.

Mark: God, that felt good! Like a burden just fell off my back. I really feel comfortable around you people.

Gil: We're glad you're here.

Judy: You better believe it! I know how hard it was for me to acknowledge that I was an alcoholic. It was a new beginning. Shit, I thought it would be the end. The pits. But I sure as hell know what you're talking about, Mark, 'cause I've been there. We all have.

Mark: Judy, I could identify with what you said earlier. I'm tired of playing out my life in bars, my lover just going along for the ride. He doesn't even drink. He's really put up with a lot of crap from me. Before we met—we've been together now a little over two years—I used to go to bars just about every night. I'd wait for some bastard to pick me up at last call or in the parking lot outside the bar. And sometimes I'd find myself in a strange motel room and wonder where in the hell I'd left my car. Well, I thought all this sleazy stuff was over when I met David, my lover. Met him at the Gay Center and we worked on a project together for weeks and he was a really great guy. Anyway, I toned down my drinking around him every time we went out together. I thought after we decided to make a commitment to each other that the 'bar scene' was behind me, but my drinking became progressively worse. He suggested that we go into therapy, see a counselor together, try to work things out. "Yeah, I've got lots of problems," I thought. "You don't really understand me, David." What I didn't want to look at was my primary problem. I was hooked on booze. I tried to get a handle on it and David tried to help, you know, cooperate in my craziness, I guess. I've just about lost David. And my job is super shaky. I'm scared, but damn it, I've been sober six whole days now and I'm beginning to feel like a human being again.

Wow! I've really talked a lot. Thanks for . . . I appreciate it.

Jack: Mark, we're here for you. For each other. I'll pass this sheet around and you take these phone numbers with you tonight and come back next week and to the other SOS meetings as well. And, although AA may not be to your liking as you said, they've got meetings in this town day and night. I want to suggest to you that you prioritize your sobriety, give yourself a chance, and go to as many meetings as you can in the first thirty days of your sobriety. At the AA meetings just screen out the parts that bother you and celebrate their sobriety. We're all in this together. Congrats again on your six days. I've been there. I know what an achievement it is.

Mark: Thank you.

Jack: Well, Fred, how's it going? We haven't heard from you tonight. Care to share with us?

Fred: I'm Fred, sober alcoholic and a pagan.

Jack: Hi, Fred.

Fred: Damn! It was good to hear you talk tonight, Mark. I've been sober sixteen years and let me tell you, the freedom from booze brings me a lot of stuff today. I know that if I were to try a little social drinking, I'd be right back on my back again. And I don't want the psycho ward anymore. Nope. I don't want sniffing through trash bins behind grocery stores for veggies. Really, I don't. Like you said at the beginning of the meeting tonight, Jack, I know what you mean. I've got a real life today. I've got an authentic life. No sheets or wires or carrots-on-sticks or spoon-bending spirits are there to keep me sober. I pay attention to my arrested disease, and by doing so I can keep it arrested.

Lots of relationships have come my way in sobriety. Some good, some so-so, some pretty lousy. And since I'm an imperfect but participating *Homo sapiens* today I like the fact that my participation in life is not fucked up by booze. Oh, I may screw things up, but I do it sober. And, since I don't see any evidence for pie in the sky, I try to be the best participant in our real world that I can be.

Yeah, relationships. I was married to a magnificent lady for fourteen years in sobriety. She never experienced me as a drunk. I met her after I'd been sober about a year. We used to live not far from here when we first got married. Yeah, Mark, I have to agree with you—gay or straight—doesn't matter, when you care for someone and you get that love back, it's hard to top. So, good luck with David. And with your new sobriety. You won't regret it. See, without sobriety I could never have met Ann. Well, we went everywhere. Started a pup farm, a kennel for German Shepherds. Now there's a dog for you.

They're full of love and full of dignity. Well, we were pretty successful in the pup business. Clients from all over the state and the country. You know, when Ann was killed about a year ago, run down by a drunk driver, I knew a drink wouldn't fix it. Life is doled out at random, and I'm grateful for our fourteen years together. Sobriety gave me that very special opportunity. I've been fortunate. I miss my gal today, but I've got the pups. Pups all around me. And I've got you people. Not a bad deal, sobriety. Mark, you hang in there. Hey, Jack, what about Karla? She hasn't done anything but hand out tissues tonight.

Jack: Thanks, Fred. Karla?

Karla: Karla, recovering "alky" and addict. Fred, I miss Ann, too. She was one hell of a lady. But we've got you, my friend. And buddy, you're pretty hot stuff yourself.

Fred: Good to be admired.

Karla: I've had a pretty good week. No complaints, really. My husband and I managed to spend a few days with some friends in Florida. The kids were pretty well-behaved and we got back alive and our house was still standing, so here I am.

Jody, our youngest, is actually speaking to her brother now. Tim seems closer to his little sister. This trip was good for the whole family. We're sure not the "Brady Bunch," but we have our moments of real togetherness. I guess I dated myself when I mentioned that ancient television series, huh? Oh well, my five years off booze and coke and pills have restored my family to me and me back to them. So they love me back and they trust me now. I can remember when they hated to see me coming. I can remember when Mommie was a 'chemical monster.' Mommie thought she was just fine at the time and that the family was the problem.

I appreciate this secular meeting. My dear godless friend Fred knows well that I am a spiritual person. I feel right at home with Fred and I love you, man. As a Buddhist, AA meetings don't meet my spiritual needs. It's a different pathway, and that's fine. I won't dwell on that; we're not here to do AA-bashing. I attend two SOS meetings a week and love 'em both. Sometimes I go to the Families and Friends group with my hubby. I've enjoyed everyone's sharing tonight. And, I might add that I feel great. I may be the happiest black lady in town.

Jack: Karla, thank you for sharing. Let's take a ten-minute break and then continue.

*   *   *

After the break, the SOS meeting is reconvened for more discussion. At the meeting's end, Jack says: "I've really enjoyed the opportunity to lead the meeting tonight.

"This meeting is self-supporting. If you can make some contribution, we will use it to help defray the cost of rent, refreshments, and other expenses." A basket is passed around.

Jack concludes the meeting: "Sobriety is our priority, and we each assume the responsibility for our lives and our sobriety. Thank you for coming, and please come back. Let's close by giving ourselves a hand for being here to support and celebrate each other's sobriety."

FROM THE NEWSLETTER

SOS members have been sharing their views by way of *The SOS Newsletter*. Published by the people who put out *Free Inquiry*, the *Newsletter* is a unique forum. This section reprints some of its most provocative articles. In order to protect anonymity of the authors, the pieces are signed here by first names only, as they are presented out of the context of a membership newsletter.

*   *   *

Treatment Or Indoctrination?

It was my first day out of detox and into the rehab program. My roommate was reading the *Big Book* of Alcoholics Anonymous, which came in the admission packet along with other AA materials.

The Twelve Steps of AA were prominently displayed across an entire wall of the lecture room. We had just finished an activity in which we were given paper and colored pencils and told to draw a picture of our "Higher Power" and then share it with the rest of the class. I sat there, between activities, thinking that I was involved in some kind of religious cult.

I had entered a fully accredited medical hospital for alcohol/drug detox and rehabilitation, but I might as well have entered a church. I attended lectures on how to turn my "will and life" over to the care of God "as I understood Him." I was told that without this "Higher Power" I had no chance of staying sober. They said that God would remove my "defects of character," which *caused* my malady in the first place, and restore me to "sanity." We began each day with a morning prayer from a book called *A Day at a Time,* and at the day's end we joined hands in a circle around lighted candles and recited the Lord's Prayer.

When I told my family that I couldn't accept this regimen of religion, they feared that I might leave and start drinking again. When I raised my objections to the counselors and therapists, I was told not to question: I had to "surrender" and "turn myself over" to the "Higher Power." They said that my thinking was getting in the way.

After twenty-eight days of "Step Study" and "Big Book Study," referred to by some as "Bible Class," I was discharged and told that I had the foundation and tools for recovery. The cost was $11,000. I left feeling frustrated, confused, and alienated. I was dismayed to find that virtually all hospitals, clinics, and other programs of recovery are based on the Twelve Step program of AA. Even the so-called scientific "aversion treatments" recommend AA to their patients.

There seemed to be no alternative—AA was the only game in town. Then I learned about a grassroots movement called Secular Organizations for Sobriety. I'm now a regular member of SOS. I no longer feel alienated, and I've found a personal recovery program that I understand and feel comfortable with. It is a privilege (rather than an obligation) to help SOS's efforts, and I view the movement as critical for those of us in need of an alternative to supernatural paths of recovery. . . .

—John W.

*   *   *

On Discrimination and Intolerance

During my recovery in a hospital-rehabilitation program, I attended classes where patients were asked to read aloud from the "Big Book" of Alcoholics Anonymous and from *Twelve Steps and Twelve Traditions*.

While I objected to many of the tenets professed in these writings, I was most disturbed by the demeaning and erroneous portrayal of the nonbeliever.

Here are some excerpts from these books which specifically address this unfortunate attitude.

Let's look first at the case of the one who says he won't believe—the belligerent one. He is in a state of mind which can be described only as savage.

Many times we talk to a new man and watch his hope rise as we discuss his alcoholic problems and explain our fellowship. But his face falls when we speak of spiritual matters, especially when we mention God, for we have reopened a subject which our man thought he had neatly evaded or entirely ignored.

Mine was exactly the kind of deep-seated block we so often see today in new people who say they are atheistic or agnostic. Their will to disbelieve is so powerful that apparently they prefer a date with the undertaker to an open-minded and experimental quest for God.

We should not talk incessantly to them about spiritual matters. They will change in time. Our behavior will convince them more than our words. We must remember that ten or twenty years of drunkeness would make a skeptic out of anyone.

The atheist may stand up in an AA meeting still denying the Deity, yet reporting how vastly he has been changed in attitude and outlook. Much experience tells us he will presently change his mind about God.

When, however, the perfectly logical assumption is suggested that underneath the material world and life as we see it, there is an All-Powerful, Guiding, Creative Intelligence, right there our perverse streak comes to the surface and we laboriously set out to convince ourselves it isn't so. We read wordy books and indulge in windy arguments, thinking we believe this universe needs no God to explain it. Were our contentions true, it would follow that life originated out of nothing, means nothing, and proceeds nowhere.

Instead of regarding ourselves as intelligent agents, spearheads of God's ever advancing Creation, we agnostics and atheists chose to believe that our human intelligence was the last word, the alpha and the omega, the beginning and the end of all. Rather vain of us, wasn't it?

We often found ourselves handicapped by obstinacy, sensitiveness, and unreasoning prejudice. Many of us have been so touchy that even casual reference to spiritual things made us bristle with antagonism. This sort of thinking had to be abandoned. Though some of us resisted, we found no great difficulty in casting aside such feelings. Faced with alcoholic destruction, we soon became as open-minded on spiritual matters as we had tried to be on other questions. In this respect alcohol was a great persuader. It finally beat us into a state of reasonableness. Sometimes this was a tedious process; we hope no one else will be prejudiced for as long as some of us were.

All this should be very encouraging news for those who recoil from prayer because they don't believe in it, or because they feel themselves cut off from God's help and direction. All of us, without exception, pass through times when we can pray only with the greatest of will. Occasionally we go even further than this. We are seized with a rebellion so sickening that we simply won't pray. When these things happen we should not think too ill of ourselves. We should simply resume prayer as soon as we can, doing what we know to be good for us.

So, practicing these Steps, we had a spiritual awakening about which finally there was no question. Looking at those who were only beginning and still doubted themselves, the rest of us were able to see the change setting in. From great numbers of such experiences, we could predict that the doubter who still claimed that he hadn't got the 'spiritual angle,' and who still considered his well-loved AA group the higher power, would presently love God and call him by name.

While AA has restored thousands of poor Christians to their churches, and has made believers out of atheists and agnostics, it has also made good AA [members] out of those belonging to the Buddhist, Islamic, and Jewish faiths.

We hope you are convinced that God can remove whatever self-will has blocked you off from him.

If you think you are an atheist, an agnostic, a skeptic, or have any other form of intellectual pride which keeps you from accepting what is in this book, I feel sorry for you.

By contrast, SOS is a friendly alternative that promotes self-reliance and free thought. We do not exist to further the cause of anything other than sobriety. There are no attempts, tacit or otherwise, to secularize anyone. Nor do we discourage others from membership in AA.

SOS respects sobriety in any form, regardless of the path one chooses.

—*John W.*

*   *   *

Consider This

I didn't take up drinking until I was twenty-one or twenty-two years old, and then only because the man who was to become my first husband had a taste for scotch. It took only five or six years for me to become a real lush. But it wasn't until I got a DUI ticket after an office party that I became concerned enough to call the National Council on Alcoholism. They referred me to an AA meeting. Typically, I thought it was all very nice for "those" people, but I was much too young to be one of "them."

Less than forty-five days later, I got a second DUI. The court gave me a choice of either thirty days in jail or three days in jail and twice-weekly AA meetings. I was no dummy—I went to the meetings. In that small town I was the youngest member. I immediately became everybody's baby, which was fine with me. I needed a lot of help. The people in that first group gave me something I'd given up on—hope. They loved me, hugged me, and listened to me babble and moan for months while I battled to stay sober.

At that time I was unconcerned about the "spiritual" aspect of the program. I'd grown up Roman Catholic, a refugee of twelve years of parochial school where one is taught to be terminally nice and not make waves. I left the church rather formally at age eighteen and at the same time gave up on organized religion, but I could not give up my "spirit-habit."

At meetings I tended to refer to my "Higher Power" as "he/she/it/they" just so I covered all the possible bases. I gladly turned my life over to the care of some mystical "force." It was easier than trying to take responsibility for it myself.

For the next eight years I managed to stay sober. I'm still not sure how I did it. I think that I got to Step Three and coasted, doing what I was told. During the second year of my sobriety, I started a young people's group and helped start a women's meeting, both revolutionary concepts for the old-liners in my home group.

I was told that if AA couldn't fix me, nothing could. Psychotherapy and medical intervention were vigorously discouraged. Everyone was adamant that I *had* to have a Higher Power, and when I balked told me that I could have any concept of "God" as I chose to understand "Him." (That inconsistency remains in AA today.) So I worked. I was on the H&I committee, held meetings at hospitals and jails, went on twelve-step calls. I wanted desperately to belong, to be a part of something.

For many years, wherever I moved, AA was always there giving me an instant support network, friends, and help.

In June 1981 I was involved in a very serious accident and spent five months in a hospital recovering from twenty-one fractures and coming to terms with an irrevocably changed life. My husband was having an affair with the upstairs neighbor. My family had a host of excuses for not coming to visit me. My father sent me one badly-typed and very brief note saying that he was sure everything would be fine because he'd given $10 to his parish priest to say a Mass for me.

All I had, and I am very grateful, were my AA friends. They kept my room filled with balloons, cards, and fruit baskets, and visited often. We even held a regular weekly meeting in my room for a while.

But even those friends caused me more pain. Though well-intentioned, their explanations for the accident were nearly always grounded in some kind of twisted religious significance. I was told, "God must love you a great deal to test you this way," and "God wants to prepare you for helping others," or "God is telling you not to be so obsessed with the physical." (I had given up smoking a year before, taken up very moderate jogging, and started an exercise class.)

All this conjecture about why the accident had happened and why I was being abandoned by those closest to me involved "God" at every turn. I came out of the hospital more agnostic than I'd ever been before. When I went to meetings, though, this line of discussion was usually quelled by quotes from the Bible. It was very clear to me that if I was going to question "God" I was no longer welcome in AA meetings.

Still, I didn't drink. But I had become an atheist and could no longer coast on AA's Step Three. I went to fewer meetings and had less and less in common with my former AA friends, most of whom shunned me as I moved away from their precious beliefs.

In the same month that I celebrated eight years of sobriety, my very much loved younger brother was brutally murdered. It proved too much for me. The day after the memorial service, I sat at my mother's kitchen table staring at a bottle of cheap brandy for half an hour before I finally decided to drink. I wanted to be numb, and then I wanted to die.

I drank for four more years after that day. Eventually, I picked up another DUI and finally decided that I needed help. More than that, I finally *wanted* it. I tried a "humanist" AA meeting in Berkeley, but it was very disappointing. The first two people who spoke praised "God" for having "kept them sober" for "X" number of years. AA had not changed.

I found a therapist who helped me decide to choose to live rather than die. And I went back to AA because it was the only game in town, the only way I knew to get sober. I went along with the mainstream out of sheer depression. I *had* to get sober again.

In the haze of my initial sobriety, I didn't give a lot of thought to the God business. My sponsor kept repeating the "personal concept" theory and gave me tapes of "New Age" meditations. Since I was desperate to get sober and belong again, I swallowed my fierce feelings and went along for the ride. But after three or four months of listening to "How It Works," I felt very isolated. I'd read Jim's article in *Free Inquiry* a year earlier and knew that there was an alternative. Although I only had a few months of sobriety, I decided I couldn't wait for someone else to start an SOS group in the Bay Area. I needed it now.

In March of [1988], we had our first sparsely attended meeting. It was gratifying beyond belief. I found I was not alone, that others shared my frustration and difficulty with AA and were looking for an alternative like SOS.

The feeling of safe, rational camaraderie is indescribable. Various AA features have proven effective, and those we use: the meetings, sharing in confidence, positive help for coping with reality. But we are able to use them rationally in SOS and do not have to take up precious time and energy with spiritual concepts we find irrelevant to the process of living sober.

Finally, I feel I have really found a home and that I belong. I don't have to compromise my beliefs to get and stay sober. I am learning how to take responsibility for my own sobriety, for my life, for my own happiness. And I smile a lot.

There is no evidence to suggest that we will ever escape comparison to AA; it is, I feel, essential that we calmly and reasonably accept this and continue to move on our own path, making use of the wealth of experience at our disposal, but always keeping in mind that we are not a clone, not a competitor, but a viable alternative. . . .

We are in the very unique position of forming this network of organizations from the bottom up. We have already given a welcome, fresh breath to many alcoholics and addicts, with both short- and long-term day-at-a-time sobriety. Our links to each other and the rest of the world should remain compassionate, rational and positive. . . .

When the first few folks who *were* SOS wrote the guide that helped me and many others start SOS meetings in our own communities, they were very clear about its secular stance.

The absence of any spiritual content whatsoever seems to me to be the whole reason for SOS's existence. But some people find that the lack of spirituality also means a lack of structure, of any clearly laid-out program, which seems to them to be antithetical to recovery. Yet for me and many others it is just this amorphous nature of SOS that offers great challenge and flexibility and personal freedom. Somewhere between anarchy and fascism is an environment of democracy, of individual freedom with responsibility, compassion, and humaneness—and that's where I think SOS ought to be in order to be a valid alternative.

I've been delighted with what such freedom can do for all of us in my own local groups. We are not bound together by ritual, dogma, steps, or traditions. But we *are* bound together by our very humanity, with all its facets, in a mutual effort toward an effective and satisfying sobriety. Staying sober is the first, last, and always priority—the bottom line. As we sober up, our minds begin to operate again and we begin to take responsibility for our sobriety. We take the credit as well. Most of us are comfortable at SOS meetings not because we speak some "code," but because we can speak freely and rationally. And that's the beauty of SOS. It is what those of us with strong secular feelings really want—freedom from booze and rational assistance in maintaining and enjoying our hard-won sobriety, as well as freedom from "programs" and "spirituality."

It was both frightening and pleasing to those of us in the two small local groups I belong to that there were no rules, no traditions, no Big Book, no format cast in stone, no program. So we periodically discuss whether to discourage "cross-talk," how to pick a chairperson, the meeting format, even the kinds and supplies of coffee and tea to have on hand. We thought about a moment of silence, but it didn't appeal to any of us for any reason, so we don't do it. We've discussed what kind of literature to have available. We've revised and then dispensed with any version of the Twelve Steps. (To some it smacks of the confession, contrition, and conversion rituals of religion.) At some time we may well bring in several versions of AA's Twelve Steps and make them available (but not mandatory, nor even strongly suggested) at meetings. The point is that it's *our* group and we can make and change the rules, letting them evolve according to the people they serve. The only real priority is sobriety.

Beyond that, secular is our name and we want to be what we say we are. As a true alternative to the spirituality of a widely available and regionally varied program we want to be a rational support network *process*. The best way seems to be to provide room for all, not promoting one way or individual but making different materials and kinds of help available for individuals to use as they can or need to.

Those of you familiar with AA may have heard of Fr. Martin's quote to the effect that every alcoholic who has been sober for twenty minutes wants to become a counselor. I went through that stage early on in AA. And one of the reasons SOS is successful for me is that I don't have any vicarious counselor

feelings here. We're all equal. No one is there to practice any
spiritual or religious or even behavioral theory. We each have
our own belief systems and it's the one safe place we can express
our secular/atheist/humanist views without fear. . . .

—*Janis G.*

*   *   *

Sobriety in the Military

I was twenty years old, stationed in Japan with the Marines,
and I was increasingly getting into trouble. I had been drinking
for five years and things were definitely not getting better. In
fact, my drinking was out of control from the very first time
I raided the family liquor cabinet, at age fifteen, until the last
hangover, nursed away with several shots of vodka the morning
after.

The Marine major who presided over my disciplinary action
as a result of some wildness committed in town sent me to
the infirmary and then to a Naval ARU (Alcoholic Rehabilitation
Unit). The usual military method of dealing with alcoholism
was to dump the addict back into civilian society. The ARU
was a pioneer experiment by the Navy, group therapy mixed
with some good old-fashioned AA.

Back at home base, I felt isolated. My hard-drinking Marine
buddies claimed I was cured and urged me to have just a few
beers with them.

Fortunately, an AA group was just getting started. It was
here that I was exposed to some of the positive aspects of

AA. The group was very small, initially no more than six members. The small size allowed intimate meetings with no peer pressure to conform to the AA "way" or finding a Higher Power. Nobody in our little group made a big deal about it.

After a year of this very isolated experience I found myself stateside, engaged with a much larger AA group. Even though I had stopped believing in a Supreme Being some years ago, I was willing to give the Higher Power business a shot because I had to stay sober no matter what. I kept waiting to get struck by the thunderbolt that was going to turn me into a believer. Alas, it never came, and I became bored with AA's mind-numbing repetition.

After leaving the military, my life was much busier and I had no use for AA for nearly ten years. When I thought of going back to AA, I cringed. I discovered SOS while reading *Free Inquiry*. Intrigued that it was located near me in Southern California, I attended the first meeting—and found only one other person there. Just like old times back in Japan.

Since those first meetings things have picked up considerably. I found many of the attractive qualities of that first AA group present in the SOS group. The style is low-key and friendly, and people are tolerant of a variety of viewpoints as there is no "official" book or literature to lean on. And most importantly, no one leans on me to force me to believe something I don't want to believe.

I'm optimistic about the future of our organization and its continued growth.

—Peter J.

*   *   *

Diversity and Tolerance:
Abandoning Conformity

The variety of alcoholics I've encountered over the years has always amazed me. Despite all the stages of alcoholism outlined in various books that I've read, there are plenty of us who don't fit into any mold. My alcoholism, for example, never fit into any pattern that I've read about in a book. I was an instant alcoholic, a reaction I've never seen addressed in the literature on alcoholism that I've read. The alcoholics that I've known have manifested their disease in so many forms that it makes me wonder just how to define what constitutes an alcoholic. The only common denominator seems to be the inability to control the intake of the substance of choice.

Our current understanding of alcoholism is that it is a complex physical and social disease. Because everybody's alcoholism is different, it is unreasonable to expect all paths to recovery to be the same. Too, people come to SOS from many social and philosophical backgrounds. At the very least, it is necessary to tolerate all types of people and their idiosyncrasies. I believe this attitude of tolerance should be more than just acceptance of peoples' quirks, though. Tolerance invites fresh ideas that can prevent stagnation. Tolerance can help us avoid the trap of dogmatism. Tolerance can help preserve the dignity of individual human belief.

SOS can reap many benefits from an atmosphere of tolerance: Diversity is important for our future growth, so our mission is best served when we reach out to as many people as possible. In a tolerant, diverse atmosphere a new person is more likely to feel comfortable. For most people the decision to do something about their problem does not come very easily, so the impression they get from the first meeting or two is critical to their decision to abstain.

With drugs of all types so widely available these days, it should come as no surprise that there are many people whose primary substance of abuse is not alcohol. Substance abusers have a lot in common with us. They, too, are missing the mechanism to use drugs in moderation. They, too, made a mess of their lives as a result of over-indulgence. In fact, it is becoming harder and harder to find abusers who abuse only a single substance. There is no need to separate the coke-heads and heroin addicts from the drunks in our meetings.

We have even known overeaters to find comfort and solace with our group. Although overeating appears to be a very different disease, the overeater will use food to deal with emotional pain just as surely as a drunk will automatically reach for a bottle. These people come to our meetings because they encounter tolerant and caring listeners, not dogmatic people telling them why they don't belong.

And lastly there are those who do believe in a God and a spiritual part of human beings. Even though I personally don't believe in a supreme being, I recognize that humans do seem to have a strong predilection to believe in some superior force. We must be careful not to trample on other people's convictions. They have a right to speak without being coerced to give up their beliefs.

Our only core belief is the need to avoid all mood-changing substances. At the moment we think our reaction to mood-altering substances is primarily related to some odd way our brains deal with these foreign substances. But who knows? In time this model of how things work may have to be modified.

It will only be through a tolerant attitude that we will continue making progress towards the understanding and treatment of this disease.

—*Peter J.*

*   *   *

Thoughts From a Newly Sober Alcoholic

I celebrated my fourth month of sobriety July 4th, 1988. When I first went to an SOS meeting I was impressed by the lack of "musts," spoken or unspoken, present in more typical twelve-step meetings. The only real and very sensible "must" I remember from my first SOS meeting was "just don't drink, *no matter what*." Making sobriety the top priority in my life is the SOS method. Everything else having to do with the quality of my life is external to this Sobriety Priority.

It really works. I sometimes feel that my use of the Sobriety Priority keeps my sobriety locked in a good strong safe—fireproof, bombproof, drunkproof.

I attend groups other than SOS for the fellowship, the sharing of experiences, and the wisdom of other people who share this disease. When it comes to it, though, I feel most comfortable in SOS.

I've put together what I call an Alcoholic's Tool-kit. It's made up of literature, tapes, thoughts, things I've seen or heard about the disease and experience of alcoholism. I use it when wanted or needed to help me keep my sobriety. It's an eclectic tool-kit—a little from here, a little from there. It's my way of staying sober, using whatever is necessary at any given time.

Nobody at SOS has told me I won't stay sober with my Alcoholic's Tool-kit and the Sobriety Priority. Nobody in SOS has told me that I should attend only SOS meetings or read only certain chosen literature pertinent to alcoholism.

The feeling I have at SOS meetings is one of freedom. I don't have to walk or talk in any way but my own way in order to be sober, as long as I remember that I have a killer disease that can never be forgotten and must be acknowledged daily.

Sobriety through SOS is a reality I can understand. Sobriety comes from *me* with a little help from my friends.

—*Larry B.*

*   *   *

Alcoholism and Sobriety: A Mixed Bag

Alcoholism is a mixed bag. The physical or genetic factors added to a multitude of other "goodies" make it a frustrating and difficult disease to get a handle on, let alone arrest.

Sobriety is a mixed bag too. It's not easy to be in a strange world "learning to live in sobriety" without the drug.

SOS is truly a safe place for people with different ways and ideas. If somebody wants to worship trees or 128 deities, or not worship at all, it's not important. There's no browbeating, no subtle or not-so-subtle pressure to conform to a particular way of life in order to have and maintain sobriety.

Rather, the spirit of SOS is the dearness and importance

of sobriety—gained by any number of means, not just accessible via one narrow road.

In my early sobriety I was uncertain about what I was going through and wished I had a guidebook to tell me common occurrences in early abstinence and give me helpful hints for especially hard times. I asked other sober alcoholics and listened closely at meetings. I developed my own guidebook, or primer out of my observations and interactions with other people. Some of the things that were helpful to me:

* While three days is the usual time for detoxification, it can sometimes take up to a week or so.

* Anxiety and depression decrease more rapidly the first three months without alcohol than in the second three months.

* Sometimes physical cravings can be lessened or stopped by niacin or lots of honey mixed with warm milk.

* Sleep patterns are disturbed often in the early days and weeks of sobriety. Dreams can be frequent and vivid.

* Associating certain life situations with alcohol consumption is common, but these associations become less strong with the passage of time in sobriety.

* Avoiding slippery situations is important. "Slippery" means something that's a stimulus for insecurity in new sobriety. It's some person, place, circumstance, or thing that an alcoholic associates with drinking.

* Vigilance and awareness of how one is in one's own sobriety at any given time is necessary to prevent the old "now-for-a-drink" pattern from taking over one's thoughts unexpectedly. It's dangerous to be lulled into a sense of security in one's sobriety just because of the amount of time one may have been sober.

* Don't take sobriety for granted. *Do* take the existence of your own alcoholism for granted. Take it "for granted" but don't forget what it means. Alcohol is a killer. It's not wise to ignore a killer.

There are troubling things that can occur in newly-found sobriety, things that aren't so scary once it's understood that similar things happen to most newly-sober alcoholics. There is also much helpful information around that can be put to use by newly-sober people who may be confused and/or experiencing things that seem frightening or strange to them.

I hope the things I've listed above are of use to other newly-sober people and I'd like to encourage them to make up a "primer" of their own based on their own individual needs. Rest assured, it *does* get better.

SOS has been instrumental in helping me to achieve and continue my sobriety. My hope is that SOS will be a place where freedom of thought is truly practiced. So if one day I "came to believe" (via brainwashing or some strange machinations of my mind, or even through the unexpected and undeniable action of a god), I would want to be able to say at an SOS meeting, "Hey, folks, I've got religion now. I'm still sober, too" and not be pressured to conform to some other way of thought. If SOS ever were to be intolerant of a person's espousal of unpopular religious or political views, then SOS would be an organization meant only for a select few. There is room for everybody in SOS as long as we keep sobriety as our first priority.

—*Larry B.*

*   *   *

Women and Sobriety

As a woman and a sober alcoholic, I have come to realize that we, as women alcoholics and addicts, are often up against unique emotional hurdles that are specific to our perception of femininity. Conventional expectations of appropriate female behavior have either consciously or subconsciously influenced both woman's response to her disease and the very nature of her addiction itself.

While a man may falsely consider that his ability to routinely consume large quantities of drugs or alcohol enhances his masculinity and bravado, a woman's sense of her own self-worth and the respect of her peers is seriously jeopardized when she begins to abuse mind-altering substances. The "female drunk" does not evoke images of "sugar and spice and everything nice." The very core of all that epitomizes traditional womanhood and femininity becomes grossly distorted when the woman herself becomes an alcoholic or drug addict.

Most women are no longer restricting their role in society soley to that of the nurturing wife and mother. However, we continue to attempt to preserve our "madonna" image by hiding our addictions by surreptitious nips from the hidden bottle in the kitchen or by discreet trips to the bathroom medicine cabinet. Even when it becomes impossible to maintain this facade any longer, we still make futile attempts to delude ourselves and deny the severity—or often even the existence—of our problem.

What may have commonly begun as the use of drugs or alcohol simply to calm the nerves, or to allay sleeplessness, has subtly developed into a full-blown addictive lifestyle. At this point the woman has two options. She may simply resign herself to her disease and become the "lush" in the neighborhood bar or the "junky" on the street. As such, she will become a non-functioning dropout from society, with nothing more than an untimely death as her fate. However, if she is willing at some point to acknowledge and accept herself for what she is, *a woman with a disease,* the process of recovery can begin. The following steps to recovery are based on my personal experience:

1. *Admit* that you have a drug or alcohol problem. If you are not sure you have one, but suspect you might, then admit it to yourself as a possibility.

2. *Accept* the fact that this addiction is a disease, a physiological disorder that can be treated. It is *not* a character flaw. It does *not* lessen your value as a woman.

3. *Seek help.* To need help in dealing with this disease is not a sign of weakness. Support-groups like SOS, often in conjunction with medical care, are needed. Talk to a medical doctor who specializes in drug/alcohol problems. An important note: Drugs and alcohol can be far more physically debilitating to women than to men.

4. *Add structure* to your daily routine. Perhaps you have become so dysfunctional that you can barely get out of bed. Whether or not this is the case, set simple daily tasks for yourself: getting up at a set hour, doing physical exercises and household chores, or keeping a daily journal. It is important to do things that you can accomplish easily, that will help to give you a sense of personal worth and well-being.

5. *Stay sober* above all else. While staying sober will not solve all your problems, it will be the basis from which you can begin to reach for the life that you want to live and to become a person you can once again respect. Sobriety is not a cure-all. It is a beginning.

*   *   *

Inundated as we are of late with the catchy "Just say no" slogan—and the television commercials promising freedom from drug and alcohol addiction in "ten days of treatment with two easy follow-ups"—we may be mistakenly led to believe that this is all it takes.

But we need to recognize that the process of "getting sober" is not the same as that of "staying sober." We cannot afford to assume that "cleaning up our act" automatically guarantees that we will "get our act together."

The initial cessation of drinking or drug-using merely removes the outer mask of our addiction. As we abruptly face ourselves in the undistorted mirror of new sobriety, we clearly see that with or without drugs and alcohol we are and always will be addicts and alcoholics.

We do not need to assume personal responsibility for the acquisition of our disease, but we certainly can claim responsibility for its daily ongoing treatment. Abstinence is essential to begin restoring self-esteem and improving our standard of living, but it will not miraculously change our personalities or resolve our problems. It *will* provide us with the impetus to learn to live with our disease.

Successful maintenance of sobriety is not an act of sheer will power. Just as the dieter will regain weight unless she restructures her eating habits, so will the sober alcoholic resume drinking unless she rehabilitates her coping skills. The process of recovery involves the conditioning of our responses to actions, reactions, and thought patterns that formerly triggered drinking behavior.

We alone are uniquely qualified to know our own needs and approach our rehabilitation accordingly. There are no absolute rights or wrongs in recovery. We must take matters into our own hands and minds and begin positive restructuring of our lives.

Sobriety must be our first priority, but the attitude with which we approach our commitment to sober living can be crucial to our recovery. Why should we be begrudgingly sober when we can set our sights high and aim for a joyous, fulfilled life of sobriety? We've heard the woeful stories: "My dog died . . . I lost my job . . . I'm so depressed . . . but thank God I'm sober." Obviously our quality of life is not contingent upon a god's good graces.

If we expend a great deal of energy thinking about the meaning or meaninglessness of life, we may lose out on the living of it. We can easily trap ourselves into an existentialist void. We cannot shield ourselves from life's unexpected blows, but neither do we need to be buffeted about by a benign, fatalistic acceptance of life's unkindness to us. None of us are immune to misfortune, illness, or death, but we can actively participate in our destiny.

We can face reality. Reality is not itself a fact. Rather, it is our own *perception* of facts that makes it "real" to us. We do not have the power to undo the past, foresee the future, nor change circumstances beyond our control, but we do have the freedom to choose the manner in which we perceive these unalterable facts. With positive perceptions, we create a reality we can face.

We can enter into a lifelong commitment to sobriety without being daunted by the seemingly endless enormity of our task. Time is just another potentially negative concept we impose upon ourselves. We need not be obsessed with remembering the past or anxiously dreading the future. Our only certainty is in the here and now. Rather than wallowing in remorseful melodramas of our past drinking, we can utilize these memories to add wisdom and experience in dealing with today. The fact that we can look beyond today and see our sobriety as a lifetime of quality living can give us the motivation to persevere.

We can learn to cope with boredom, loneliness, fear, rejection, stress, and anger. We can live soberly with the unfairness and unknowns that are innately part of our humanness. We can even take delight and find humor in our human fallibility. Whatever each moment holds for us, we can live it to the fullest with a zestful sense of adventure.

We fortify ourselves with sober minds and bodies and courageously embrace the uncertainties of our existence. In sobriety we do not seek to escape from life, but to enter into the experience of living.

—Jeannine B.

*   *   *

An Al-Anon Experience

"Al-Anons are sicker than the alcoholics."

This was the first and very clear message I received from my Al-Anon/AA contacts. It appeared to be a great source of humor for many, but I was angry at its judgmental tone. In this sudden grouping as a "sick Al-Anon," none of my individuality was acknowledged.

The alcoholic in my life had a relapse in the spring of 1987, requiring hospitalization in a rehab program. During this hospitalization Al-Anon was suggested, and I realized that although I was not an alcoholic I had a lot of work to do. I had finally begun to understand that alcoholism is a family disease. We are all affected.

Thirty meetings in thirty days would provide the necessary groundwork for my own recovery. A demanding and chaotic work schedule was no excuse, and I was discouraged from using my own judgment in my daily life as my judgment was affected by my significant other's drinking. (At this point I *was* beginning to question my judgment!)

One evening I attended a Step Study to discuss the Third Step, which states: "Made a decision to turn our will and our lives over to the care of God as we understood Him."

I heard many people say that they had a dialogue with their God every morning, and he let them know what would be right for the day.

My head began to spin. As I began to raise my hand, an older woman was acknowledged.

"What if you don't have a God?" she asked.

No God? Hands shot up, speakers eagerly requested recognition.

"You are spiritually bankrupt," said a young woman. "After you've been in the program awhile you'll feel God's presence. I felt just like you when I entered Al-Anon, but now I speak with God every day and I know He's with me all the time. I just turn my life over to God and know he'll make the right decision for me."

And yet they insist that Al-Anon is not a religion.

There are those of us who don't have a god and do not desire a god in our life. This does not make us any less able to grow and learn from our experiences and the experience of others.

There may be family members and friends who are *not* "sicker than the alcoholic." And there may be times when we are. Nevertheless, we must have contact and support from people who've been through similar experiences but who allow us to have our own version of our life experience and do not judge or restrain our dealings with our own experience. There must be more than one way to reach a solution. And there must be a place for those of us who choose not to seek a god to direct us through our day.

—Barbara B.

A POSTSCRIPT

I was just about to put the finishing touches to this book when the phone rang and an old friend invited me to take a break and accompany him to a favorite restaurant of his in another part of the city. It would be his treat. I accepted, and he came by about two hours later. Enroute to the place, we laughed a lot and reminisced about old times, old friends. Traffic was heavy, so we parked on a side street off the main drag.

As we got out of his car, two figures emerged from the darkness and pointed guns in our faces. "See this! Give me your money, motherfucker," said one.

"Do like he says, shithead!" said his companion, as he shoved my friend back toward the hood of his car. My half of the hold-up team was distressed when he shook out the contents of my wallet. As cards cascaded onto the pavement he glared at me, realizing I had no cash. "Where's your money, fuckface?" He pointed his gun at my face.

I looked him in the eye with that respectful calmness that can come with shock and said, "I don't have any money, man." I raised my arms in the air and said, "Here, search me if you want." He ripped a pack of cigarettes from my shirt pocket

My friend's voice seemed to come from far away: "Honest, sir, he doesn't have any money. I've got the money. Here, take it."

The assailant's companion yelled, "Now get the fuck out of here—move, go, now!" My assailant echoed his friend's sentiments and we ran across the street, dodging cars in the night.

"They took my car!"

"What else?"

"Thirty dollars in cash, my wallet, credit cards. . ."

"I'm so sorry. . . ."

"We're alive! We're lucky they didn't shoot us!"

"Yeah."

When the police finally arrived, they weren't exactly the "care squad."

A neighbor took us back to my friend's house, where we fell asleep about 4 A.M., after talking for hours. The small bedroom my friend had provided for me was next to louvered windows, so he loaned me a hammer to keep by my bedside, as his address was in the hands of the perpetrators. He took a large kitchen knife to his bedroom.

In the morning I returned home by bus. There, the reality of the incident hit me, and I felt violated, frightened, fortunate, weak, crazy, guilty, angry, sad, hurt, and anxious. But I also felt profoundly victorious: They could not take my sobriety. I had no urge to drink. My sobriety was protected.

Life can be full of nasty surprises. Of this we can be certain.

As a sober alcoholic, I say booze won't make them better, or make them go away. Sobriety, however, can make them better. Of this we can also be certain, every day.

NOTES

1. *Alcoholics Anonymous* (New York: Alcoholics Anonymous World Services, 1976), 59–60.

2. Kathleen Whalen FitzGerald, Ph.D., *Alcoholism: The Genetic Inheritance* (New York: Doubleday, 1988), 7, 10.

3. Kathleen Cahill Tsubata, "The Low-Down On Addiction" in *The World & I* (Washington, D.C.: The Washington Times Corp., Nov., 1988), 324–325.

4. George E. Vaillant, *The Natural History of Alcoholism* (Cambridge: Harvard University Press, 1983), 314.

5. Vaillant, 313.

6. Tom Dardis, *The Thirsty Muse: Alcohol and the American Writer* (New York: 1989).

7. David D. Burns, M.D., *Feeling Good: The New Mood Therapy* (New York: Signet Books, 1980), 40–41.

REFERENCES/RESOURCES

Alcoholism: The Genetic Inheritance
Kathleen Whalen FitzGerald, Ph.D.
Doubleday
Bantam Doubleday Dell Publishing Group, Inc.
666 Fifth Avenue
New York, New York 10103

The Natural History of Alcoholism: Causes, Patterns, and Paths to Recovery
Dr. George E. Vaillant
Harvard University Press
79 Garden Street
Cambridge, Massachusetts 02138

Under the Influence: A Guide to the Myths and Realities of Alcoholism
Dr. James R. Milam and Katherine Ketcham
Bantam Books, Inc.
666 Fifth Avenue
New York, New York 10103

Free Inquiry
Published quarterly by the
Council for Democratic and Secular Humanism
Post Office Box 5
Buffalo, New York 14215

Freethought Today
Published by the Freedom from Religion Foundation
Post Office Box 750
Madison, Wisconsin 53701

Feeling Good: The New Mood Therapy
David D. Burns, M.D.
Signet Books
NAL Penguin, Inc.
1633 Broadway
New York, New York 10019

Secular Organizations for Sobriety
SOS Clearinghouse
Post Office Box 15781
North Hollywood, California 91615

Priority One
Outpatient Chemical Dependency Treatment Program
Post Office Box 46248
Los Angeles, California 90046

Biological Basis of Alcoholism
Yedy Israel and Jorge Mardones (1971)
John Wiley & Sons, Inc.
Wiley-Interscience
New York, New York

The Alcoholisms: Detection, Diagnosis and Assessment
George R. Jacobson, Ph.D. (1976)
Human Sciences Press
Behavioral Publications, Inc.
72 Fifth Avenue
New York, New York 10011

The Disease Concept of Alcoholism
E. M. Jellinek (1960)
College and University Press
New Haven, Connecticut
in association with Hill House Press
New Brunswick, New Jersey

Alcoholism: A Treatment Manual
Wayne Poley, Ph.D., Gary Lea, M.A., Gail Vibe, M.A. (1979)
Gardner Press, Inc.
New York, New York
Dist. by Halsted Press
(a division of John Wiley & Sons, Inc.)
New York, New York

The Female Alcoholic: A Social Psychological Study
Barry A. Kinsey, Ph.D. (1966)
Bannerstone House
301-327 E. Lawrence Ave.
Springfield, Illinois

How to Stubbornly Refuse to Make Yourself Miserable About Anything, Yes Anything!
Albert Ellis, Ph.D. (1988)
Lyle Stuart, Inc.
120 Enterprise Ave.
Secaucus, New Jersey 07094

A New Guide to Rational Living
Albert Ellis, Ph.D. and R. A. Harper (1975)
Wilshire Books
North Hollywood, California

Is Alcoholism Heriditary?
Donald Goodwin, M.D. (1976)
Oxford University Press
New York, New York

The Diagnosis & Treatment of Alcoholism
Edited by Jack H. Mendelson, M.D. and Nancy K. Mello, Ph.D.
(1985)
McGraw-Hill Book Co.
New York, New York

Frontiers of Alcoholism
Edited by Morris E. Chafetz, M.D., Howard T. Blane, Ph.D.,
and Marjorie J. Hill, Ph.D. (1970)
Science House
New York, New York

Alcoholism Mechanisms and Management
Max Hayman, M.D. (1966)
Charles C. Thomas, Publisher
Bannerstone House
301-327 E. Lawrence Ave.
Springfield, Illinois

Medical Disorders of Alcoholism: Pathogenesis and Treatment
Charles S. Lieber, M.D. (1982)
W.B. Saunders Co.
West Washington Square
Philadelphia, Pennsylvania 19105

The Origin of Consciousness in the Breakdown of the Bicameral Mind
Julian Jaynes, Ph.D. (1982)
Houghton Mifflin Co.
Boston, Massachusetts

Prometheus Books
Free catalogue offers books on philosophy, ethics, science, humanism, free thought, education, social science, religion, the paranormal, and more.
700 East Amherst Street
Buffalo, New York 14215

Exuberance: A Philosophy of Happiness
Paul Kurtz
Prometheus Books
700 East Amherst Street
Buffalo, New York 14215